A New Version in English Verse

by

BARRY KORNHAUSER

Adapted from

Cyrano de Bergerac

by

Edmond Rostand

To Jessy & Rick whose kindness and generosity are only exceeded by their PANACHE! with gratitude, esteem, and affection, — Barry

Dramatic Publishing

Woodstock, Illinois • England • Australia • New Zealand

*** NOTICE ***

The amateur and stock acting rights to this work are controlled exclusively by THE DRAMATIC PUBLISHING COMPANY without whose permission in writing no performance of it may be given. Royalty must be paid every time a play is performed whether or not it is presented for profit and whether or not admission is charged. A play is performed any time it is acted before an audience. Current royalty rates, applications and restrictions may be found at our website: www.dramaticpublishing.com, or we may be contacted by mail at: DRAMATIC PUBLISHING COMPANY, 311 Washington St., Woodstock IL 60098.

COPYRIGHT LAW GIVES THE AUTHOR OR THE AUTHOR'S AGENT THE EXCLUSIVE RIGHT TO MAKE COPIES. This law provides authors with a fair return for their creative efforts. Authors earn their living from the royalties they receive from book sales and from the performance of their work. Conscientious observance of copyright law is not only ethical, it encourages authors to continue their creative work. This work is fully protected by copyright. No alterations, deletions or substitutions may be made in the work without the prior written consent of the publisher. No part of this work may be reproduced or transmitted in any form or by any means, electronic or mechanical, including photocopy, recording, videotape, film, or any information storage and retrieval system, without permission in writing from the publisher. It may not be performed either by professionals or amateurs without payment of royalty. All rights, including, but not limited to, the professional, motion picture, radio, television, videotape, foreign language, tabloid, recitation, lecturing, publication and reading, are reserved.

For performance of any songs, music and recordings mentioned in this play which are in copyright, the permission of the copyright owners must be obtained or other songs and recordings in the public domain substituted.

©MMIII by
BARRY KORNHAUSER
Revisions and new material ©MMVIII

Printed in the United States of America
All Rights Reserved
(CYRANO)

ISBN 1-58342-163-7

For

my children
Max, Sam, Ariel

my wife
Carol Anne

my mother
Florence

with love lots larger than Cyrano's nose

Also for

Gayle Sergel

Char Borman

Kim Bennett

and especially

Michael D. Mitchell

"C'est à vous que je le dédie."

IMPORTANT BILLING AND CREDIT REQUIREMENTS

All producers of the play *must* give credit to the author of the play in all programs distributed in connection with performances of the play and in all instances in which the title of the play appears for purposes of advertising, publicizing or otherwise exploiting the play and/or a production. The name of the author *must* also appear on a separate line, on which no other name appears, immediately following the title, and *must* appear in size of type not less than fifty percent (50%) the size of the title type. Biographical information on the author, if included in the playbook, may be used in all programs. *In all programs this notice must appear:*

"Produced by special arrangement with
THE DRAMATIC PUBLISHING COMPANY of Woodstock, Illinois"

All producers of *Cyrano* must include the following acknowledgment on the title page of all programs distributed in connection with performances of the play and on all advertising and promotional materials:

"*Cyrano* was commissioned and produced by the
Fulton Opera House in Lancaster, Pennsylvania."

Cyrano was first performed at the Fulton Opera House in Lancaster, Pennsylvania, September 21-October 1, 2000.

Cyrano de Bergerac . . . . KIM BENNETT
Roxane. . . . . MELISSA CHALSMA
Christian de Neuvillette. . . . . TRENT DAWSON
Comte de Guiche . . . . KEVIN WALDRON
Le Bret. . . . . MARK MINEART
Ragueneau . . . . GEORGE HOSMER
Bellerose/Musketeer/Capuchin/Spaniard . . . . JON SHAVER
Montfleury/Apprentice 3/Mother Marguerite. . ROBERT BROCK
Duenna/Sister Claire . . . . TERRI MASTROBUONO
Vicomte de Valvert/Apprentice 2/Cadet 7 . . . . . ALVIN KEITH
Cut-Purse/Apprentice 1/Sentry. . . . . BRIAN MARTIN
Orange Girl/Lise/Sister Marthe. . . . . DANA P. DIMON
Musician 1/Page 1/Cadet 5/Nun . . . . SPIFF WEIGAND
Musician 2/Page 2/Cadet 6/Nun . . . . MICHAEL DROLET
Cadet 1/Spaniard. JASON ADAMO
Cadet 2/Spaniard . . . . MICHAEL JOHN CASEY
Cadet 3 . . . . NICHOLAS LONGOBARDI
Cadet 4 . . . . JOE THOMPSON

Other Assorted Citizens/Spaniards/Voice of Jodelet. . . . .
JONATHAN GROFF, ERIC & STEPHEN DIEHL

Director . . . . MICHAEL D. MITCHELL
Costume Designer . . . . BETH DUNKELBERGER
Scenic Designer . . . . ROBERT KLINGELHOEFER
Lighting Designer . . . . BILL SIMMONS
Original Music & Sound Design. . . . . RON BARNETT
Stage Manager. . . . . DANIEL G. WALCZYK
Fight Choreographer. . . . . JANE RIDLEY
Hair/Makeup Consultant . HEATHER MACDONALD JOHNSON
Casting . . . . JUDY HENDERSON C.S.A., New York City

CYRANO

A Play in Two Acts

<u>CHARACTERS</u>
(See casting notes in back of book for doubling, tripling suggestions.)

CYRANO DE BERGERAC
ROXANE
CHRISTIAN DE NEUVILLETTE
RAGUENEAU
COMTE DE GUICHE
LE BRET
DUENNA
VICOMTE DE VALVERT
CADETS (7)
BELLEROSE
ORANGE GIRL
CUT-PURSE
MONTFLEURY
APPRENTICES (3)
LISE
MAN OF LETTERS
MUSICIANS (2)
MUSKETEERS (2)
PAGES (2)
CAPUCHIN
SENTRY
MOTHER MARGUERITE
SISTER CLAIRE
SISTER MARTHE
NUNS
SPANIARDS
VOICE OF JODELET

About the Poetry (or "A Verse-Case Scenario")

There were a number of reasons for writing this adaptation of Cyrano de Bergerac in verse. Firstly, the choice was intended to honor Rostand's original, a work written in iambic hexameter Alexandrines, the style of the great classical French dramatists. Secondly, the use of rhyme serves to acknowledge, perhaps even bolster, the critical nature of poetry itself in the story of the play. The lives of the characters are driven and transformed by words, and it seemed only appropriate to emphasize their very presence in the text. Thirdly, the play is not a realistic one. It portrays a world both romantic and somewhat idealized. The verse helps elevate the piece beyond everyday reality. Finally, this use of language offers opportunities to capture a bit of the true spirit of Rostand, with its rich humor all too often neglected in many adaptations. Rostand's own word play was delightful, and his masterwork, *Cyrano de Bergerac,* is as funny as it is moving.

That said, a note of caution about the performers' reading of this poetry might be in order. With language there is always a constant battle between the music of the words and their meaning. It should be the goal of director and actors to make the text read as naturalistically as possible, speaking the lines with the quality of ordinary speech, so that the rhyming all but disappears, leaving only a suggestion of it in the audiences' ears.

"It's as if someone pumped nitrous oxide into the theater, so giggly and woozy are the goings-on. ... An intensely moving treatise on not only the alchemic powers of love but also the beauty found in sacrifice."

— *The Washington Times*

"A frothy 'Cyrano' invigorated by ... the irreverence of a zinger-packed adaptation ... that performs a kind of teasing gavotte on the ears. ... Packs surprising punch."

— *The Washington Post*

"For years I wanted to direct a production [of *Cyrano de Bergerac*] that captured its wit, poetry and passion. When I read the adaptation by Barry Kornhauser, I knew I had finally found an English version in verse that retained the rich humor and beauty of Rostand's play. ... Tremendously literate, tremendously clever ... this adaptation has the modernity that you want in a new translation and yet doesn't sacrifice the classicism."

— *Michael Kahn, Artistic Director*
The Shakespeare Theatre

Act I

Scene i: A Performance at the Hotel de Bourgogne.

*(The curtain opens revealing the Hall of the Hotel de
Bourgogne in 1640 Paris. Upstage center is a proscenium
arch, framing a small stage concealed for now behind an or-
nate curtain, perhaps decorated with an array of huge fleurs
de lis. Two unlit chandeliers hang low, and a row of unlit
footlights transverse the downstage floor of this "replica"
theater. A bench sits on a diagonal at each side of this stage
– the cheap seats. As the actual theater's main drape completes its rise, four cadets enter from the back of the house,
two per aisle. Simultaneously, Bellerose, carrying a lantern,
makes a panicky entrance through the central slit in the small
stage's curtain. He is followed by two of his company's musicians whose playing becomes a part of the grander orchestration underscoring this opening.)*

BELLEROSE *(to an imagined curtain-puller high
in the wings)*: No, not yet! You're early! *(And to the
actual audience and the approaching cadets)* Go away!
                              The play doesn't start until two.

CADET 1 *(reaching the stage,
along with the others)*: Well then, while we are waiting,
                              we will just have to find something to do.

9

BELLEROSE: Tranquil and refined,
                      if you do not mind,
                            sirs.

CADET 3 *(holding up a deck)*: I have cards!

CADET 4 *(shaking a clenched hand
                    as if rolling dice)*: Here are dice!

BELLEROSE: Please!

CADET 2 *(to 1)*:   Some sword *play* would be nice
                              in prelude to the drama.

   *(Cadets 1 and 2 draw their swords
    and pose to begin fencing.)*

BELLEROSE: Dear gentlemen, I am a-
                      fraid not. House rules, you see. No fights.

CADET 1:   Bellerose…

BELLEROSE: Yes?

CADET 1:   Go light your lights.

   (Cadets 1 and 2 playfully threaten him with their foils.)

BELLEROSE: Very well then. But I'll first collect your
   admission fee.

CADET 2:   Not a sou; we get in free.

BELLEROSE: Really? And why, pray tell, might that be?

CADET 1:   Why!? Because we are the Cadets...

ALL FOUR CADETS: ...of Gascony!

*(Cadets 1 and 2 poke Bellerose lightly in the belly
with their swords.)*

BELLEROSE: "Point" taken!

*(He falls back into the waiting arms of the other two Cadets
who lift him under his arms and carry him upstage, his legs
flailing the air.)*

MUSICIAN 1 *(tuning his instrument)*:   How's that?

MUSICIAN 2:   Still *notably* flat.

*(1 grudgingly resumes his tuning as Bellerose begins lighting
the chandeliers and the footlights, a business that can occupy
much of his upcoming time. Cadets 3 and 4 sit on a bench
and begin playing cards. 1 and 2 practice dueling. Others begin entering. From a wing comes the Cut-Purse. And again
down the aisle of the house, Christian and Ragueneau, the
latter carrying a period container of baked goods, the former
casting his eyes all about the auditorium. Down the opposite
aisle comes the Orange Girl, hawking her wares to the audience. [Throughout the scene, all of these characters must
stay busy. Much of their business is suggested, but more can
be created. For example, the musicians continue to tune their
instruments, a cadet juggles the Orange Girl's fruits, etc.]).*

ORANGE GIRL *(moving down the aisle)*: Oranges!
                              Freshly squeezed lemonade!
                    For long-time subscribers, prunes pureed!

BELLEROSE *(to the Cut-Purse, interrupting his work
    of illuminating the theater)*: Monsieur, your pay, please.

                                                    Fifteen sous.

CUT-PURSE: Yes, of course. A moment or two.

    (He slinks away.)

ORANGE GIRL: I have homemade macaroons to sell!

RAGUENEAU: Might I have instead a muscatel?
    *(She nods and prepares one for him as he
    continues to Christian.)* Well, this is it –
    the famed Hotel de Bourgogne!
    You don't know Paris, my boy, if you don't know this stage -
    which, at two, will present the debut of "La Clorise"
                    by Balthasar Baro –

BELLEROSE: - who is all the rage
                    just now. You'll find his play
    as sharp *(rubbing his previously poked stomach)* as an épée.
        Baro is a true poet, not a faker
        like this pretentious prosaic baker

                                    at your side.
            (Ragueneau begins to protest.) Good to see you,
    Ragueneau. *(Ragueneau is appeased, until)* I missed my lunch.

ORANGE GIRL: Right here, people;
                    quench your thirst with delicious Empire Punch!

RAGUENEAU *(handing over
    the container to Bellerose)*: Voila; my usual culinary pittance.
                    Sufficient, I do trust, to gain the admittance
    of both this fine boy and myself.

BELLEROSE: It's good that my heart is soft, sir,
                                    because your rolls are hard.

(He taps one against Ragueneau's forehead.)

CADET 1 *(thrusting his foil lightly on 2's chest)*: Ah, a hit!

CADET 2: I admit.

(They resume.)

RAGUENEAU: Then you accept?

BELLEROSE: I do. Though not for you, you old baker cum bard,
    but for this charming newcomer.
                                    Who is he, a fresh apprentice?
        (Pulling Christian aside) A word, mon cher, to the wise
about your cheeky master. This breadmaker's songs
                    are like his yeast – they only serve to get a rise.

RAGUENEAU: Some director! You've no ear for poetry;
                    less an eye for bonhomie, my foolish Bellerose.
This new arrival to our fair city is the *Baron* de Neuvillette –

BELLEROSE: who has come for a dose
    of culture! Bravo, *Baron*. ...Baron?
    (But Christian's attentions have wandered again.
                    To Ragueneau) Has he heard anything I said?

RAGUENEAU: I would guess not a single word, monsieur,
                                    for you have sorely misread
    this open book. Although Christian and I are only newly met,
I can tell you he hungers neither for your art nor my Crépe Suzette.
    Why, don't you see, his attentions lie not on the stage,
    but on "dramas" more pertinent to young men his age.

BELLEROSE: Alas, another youth succumbs to temptations
(indicating large breasts with his hands)…weighty,
the hunt and pursuit of the fabled Parisian lady.
Well, there are none like –

ORANGE GIRL *(offering one to Christian)*: Madeleine?

(He declines politely.)

RAGUENEAU *(nudging him)*:   Christian! Regard.

CHRISTIAN: Sir? Oh, sorry. *(To Bellerose)* No, monsieur.
I've come with the Guard,
to join the ranks of the *Gascon* Cadets.

BELLEROSE: Then, Baron, you have my deepest regrets.
The Cadets have been known –
*(He turns to point at the dueling Cadets just in time to catch
the Cut-Purse nimbly stealing the purse of one of them.
Neither Christian or Ragueneau have noticed. He smiles.)*
- to suffer losses…in those ranks.
But time for the show.
(Indicating the container) As always, Ragueneau, my thanks.

RAGUENEAU: Bon appetit.

BELLEROSE: Please, take a seat.

CUT-PURSE *(counting coins out of the
Cadet's purse)*: Bellerose! Your fifteen sous.

BELLEROSE: Make that thirty for you.
(Gesturing toward the duelists) I know the Gascon bank
from which you newly withdrew.

(Bellerose is reluctantly paid.)

ORANGE GIRL: Sweet raspberry syrup!

BELLEROSE *(completing his candle lighting,*
                    calling): Raise the chandelier up!
  (Nothing.) Jodelet?!

VOICE OF JODELET: You want fast work,
  pay a fair wage! "Heads" on stage!

(The first chandelier begins to rise into playing position.)

CHRISTIAN: Dear Ragueneau, I don't see her anywhere!
  You said all of Paris' Precieux would be here.

RAGUENEAU: Of course, my boy; it is, after all,
                                    a Baro premiere.
But you say you saw her just once in passing.
                            Are you sure to recognize her?

CHRISTIAN: You would need not ask that question if,
                    like me, you had gazed into her eyes, sir.
    They have stayed in mine
                    since our glances met that fateful day that I arrived.
  And now, my friend and guide, with you here by my side,
                            I shall not be deprived
of the chance to learn who she is,
    for I'm told you know everyone – be they from town or court.
All come into your bake shop –

RAGUENEAU: – where I "cook-up" my wicked songs
                            about them, making such sport
    of all their lives.

CHRISTIAN: Which is why you must "sing out" her name
                                    when she appears!

RAGUENEAU: And I will do so loud and clear, my boy,
                                    so allay all of your fears.
If –

CHRISTIAN: *When!* –

RAGUENEAU: she arrives, you will not think any less of me.
                    I shall make her as familiar as a favorite recipe.

CHRISTIAN: Praise heaven above,
                    I was directed to your patisserie, kind sir.

(He embraces Ragueneau vigorously.)

RAGUENEAU: Enough of that. Eyes back to earth,
                    dear boy, or however shall we find her.

*(They both look about the audience. As they do so,
Bellerose notices a new arrival and rushes to collect
his admission fee.)*

BELLEROSE: Welcome, sir, you can pay right here.

MUSKETEER 1:   I don't pay. I'm a Musketeer.

BELLEROSE: But –

MUSKETEER 1 *(spotting the Orange Girl)*:
    Besides, I've only come to collect a "souvenir."

ORANGE GIRL: May I serve you, sir?

MUSKETEER 1:   Avec plaisir.
  Just give me a moment, won't you, to examine your "wares."

*(He studies her tray. Of course, her chest happens to be in
the way.)*

BELLEROSE *(to self)*: Ah well, don't care for our plays?
                            Then try our concessionaires.
  *(Returning to Christian and Ragueneau who are
  still perusing the crowd)* Just so long as they do fill the seats,
                            and hence the lines on my balance sheets.
                        Yes, we have quite the audience today.

RAGUENEAU: The whole Academy, *(pointing)* even Corneille!

BELLEROSE *(to Christian)*: Well, the play features,
                            of course, the great Montfleury.

RAGUENEAU: A casting decision that does tempt destiny.
                    Just do not be surprised, Bellerose,
                    that if he opens, you forthwith close.

BELLEROSE: Such utter drivel. Says who?

RAGUENEAU: Only my good friend - *Cyrano de Bergerac*!

*(The musical underscoring comes to a screeching halt
at the mention of the name. So do all other sounds
and actions, at least momentarily.)*

BELLEROSE: What?

RAGUENEAU: Yes, if Montfleury dares take the stage,
                    Cyrano vows to give him the sack.

LE BRET *(entering the back of the house)*: And *that* is the spectacle I'm here to enjoy.

RAGUENEAU *(to Christian)*: Your commander.

BELLEROSE *(whispering)*:   One of the Gascon hoi polloi,
       I'm afraid, not to mention a grump.
  So polish that boot. *(Christian wipes it
  on the back of his pants leg.)* And watch your rump.

  (He swats Christian's behind.)

RAGUENEAU: Bellerose, don't even start.

BELLEROSE: Oh, Ragueneau, have –

CADET 3 *(revealing a card triumphantly)*:   A heart!

CUT-PURSE *(clutching the Orange Girl)*: A kiss?

CADET 1 *(again jabbing 2 with his foil)*:   A hit!

  *(The Orange Girl tries to slap the
  Cut-Purse. He ducks out of the way.)*

CUT-PURSE: A miss!

  (She steps on his foot.)

CADET 2 *(responding to the jab)*:   You twit.

CUT-PURSE: My toe!

ORANGE GIRL: De trop! *["Not wanted"]*

CUT-PURSE *(stealing Bellerose's purse)*: Thirty sous? Say "adieu."
                              Oh, and interest does accrue.

LE BRET *(arriving on the stage)*:   Ragueneau!

RAGUENEAU: Le Bret!

LE BRET (*grudgingly handing coins to
  Bellerose who intercepts his approach)*: Cyrano?

RAGUENEAU *(shrugging)*:   Not yet.
              But, a new recruit – de Neuvillette.
         Christian, this is your Captain, Le Bret.

CHRISTIAN *(with a bow)*: Monsieur.

LE BRET: Monsieur. So when did you reach Paris, Cadet?

CHRISTIAN: Exactly a fortnight ago; that I'll not forget.
  (To Ragueneau) It was the first time I saw *her*.

LE BRET: "Her?"

RAGUENEAU: Best not get him started, sir.

  (Ragueneau turns Christian's head back toward Le Bret.)

LE BRET: So, you'll be joining our noble ranks,
  de Neuvillette.

CHRISTIAN: Tomorrow, Captain.

BELLEROSE *(to self, lamenting)*:   So soon
  such youth and beauty taken to the front.

LE BRET: But first to the *front* row! This afternoon
  be sure to grab a good seat, Cadet. It should be quite the show.

RAGUENEAU: That is, of course,
                                presuming the appearance of Cyrano.

LE BRET *(gruffly)*: Oh, he will be here, cake-maker,
                                        that without fail.

  (And with a change of tone) So Christian,
                        from where in Gascony do you hail?

CHRISTIAN: I don't, sir. I come from the Loire,
                                the town of Touraine.

BELLEROSE: Oh, mon dieu.
                  Yet more cause for Cyrano to complain.

CHRISTIAN: What? Why?   …Just who is this "Cyrano?"

LE BRET: You don't know!?

CHRISTIAN: Well, not exactly.

LE BRET: Holy Mother of God.
  And this he admits so matter of factly!
  "Who – is – Cyrano?" Tell me,
  Ragueneau, is this fresh young friend of yours making fun?

RAGUENEAU *(to Christian)*: "Who is Cyrano?"
                  Why only the most remarkable being under the sun.

LE BRET: And moon!

CHRISTIAN: Forgive me; I am new to Paris.

LE BRET: Yes, but surely his reputation transcends
  our gates.

RAGUENEAU: He is only the rarest,

LE BRET: choisest,

RAGUENEAU: soul on earth.

LE BRET: Not to mention the best of friends,

RAGUENEAU: and the bravest of men.

MUSICIAN 1:   A Poet!

CUT-PURSE: Philosopher!

MUSICIAN 2:   Scholar!

BELLEROSE: There's no wit
  like him!

CADET 1:   He is the first among -

CADET 2 *(with arm around 1)*:   - our tight coterie.

CHRISTIAN: And you are...?

CADET 3:   Need you ask?!

ALL CADETS *(raising their swords)*: The Cadets of Gascony!

CHRISTIAN *(pointing to himself)*: Well then, -

CADET 4 *(paying no mind)*: Soldier and Swordsman
                                        Extraordinaire!

ORANGE GIRL: And, oh, oh, Monsieur, above all –
                                        what Savoir Faire!

MUSKETEER 1 *(a bit jealous)*: Ha!

LE BRET: You disagree, sir?

MUSKETEER 1:   No! Au contraire.
                  He has certain "features" beyond compare.

LE BRET: Yes, bigger than life, our Cyrano is!

RAGUENEAU: Especially...

ALL *(in a whisper)*:   ...his nose.

RAGUENEAU *(confidentially to Christian)*: And,
  if you ever saw it, you would even say it glows.

LE BRET: Glows?

  *(They stare intently at each other, face to face.
  Then both nod their heads in a sort of confirmation.)*

BELLEROSE: Still, his sword will slice in half
                          all who find it cause to laugh.

LE BRET *(looking about)*: But where the devil is he?!

CHRISTIAN *(also looking, but stopping, stunned)*:   There!

(He is staring at the upper box, house right, which Roxane has just entered along with her Duenna, the Comte de Guiche and the Vicomte de Valvert.)

RAGUENEAU: You've spotted Cyrano? Where? Where?

CHRISTIAN: No, not your de Bergerac. But...*her!*

(He points to Roxane in the box.)

LE BRET *(rolling his eyes, and with a dismissive gesture)*: I best go find him. It's a large theater.
                                                And there is far too little time.

(Reminded, Bellerose signals the crew to raise the second chandelier. Le Bret exits.)

CHRISTIAN: Who is she?

RAGUENEAU: Your taste is sublime.
   That is Madeleine Robin, called Roxane...

CHRISTIAN: Heaven-sent.

RAGUENEAU: Indeed. Elegant, artistic and...intelligent.

CHRISTIAN *(unsettled by that prospect)*: Alas!

RAGUENEAU: No, Roxane cannot be matched.

CHRISTIAN: So beautiful.

RAGUENEAU: And so unattached...

CHRISTIAN: But who is that with her – that man?

RAGUENEAU: Ha! The Comte de Guiche with his cordon bleu.
In love with her, but *very* married –
                    to the niece of Cardinal Richelieu.
Which is why he is pressing Roxane
to wed his noblesse flunky.

(Ragueneau indicates the other nobleman in de Guiche's party.)

CHRISTIAN: Why? And who is he?

RAGUENEAU: That is the uninspiring
        Vicomte de Valvert who will complacently agree
to allow de Guiche to carry out his heart's every dark desire,
making the young lady's situation, to say the least, quite -

CHRISTIAN: Dire!
      Has the man no honor?

RAGUENEAU: What need? He has prestige.

CHRISTIAN: And so poor Roxane is under a shameful siege.

RAGUENEAU: Yes, and with the Comte bent on conquest,
                all is certainly without hope lest
he be somehow stopped for, 'though she continues to resist,
          de Guiche indubitably has the power to insist
        upon his way. *(Christian begins to draw his sword.)*
No, Christian, stay!
                I have exposed his wicked intention
                 in a recent song of my invention.
And as is my reckless pension, I sing it daily in my shop.

CHRISTIAN: Ah.

RAGUENEAU: Need I even mention –

CHRISTIAN: that he would prefer for you to stop.

RAGUENEAU: Quite! But look here, Christian;
what is this I see? Valvert watching Roxane watching *you* despite
    his clear unease. *(Christian stares back at Roxane, as
    Ragueneau notices something else, quite unnerving.)*
  Oh, and - ha - *I* seem to be the target
                        on which de Guiche has aimed *his* sight!
Um, if you please, suddenly I've an urge to go out for a drink.
    Care to join me? Tout suite.
        (Not waiting for an answer) Whate'er. Feel free.

    (He exits hastily.)

CHRISTIAN *(still staring at Roxane)*: I will stay here, I think.

    *(Taking advantage of Christian's distraction, the Cut-Purse
    sneaks up behind him. Meanwhile de Guiche has noticed the
    mutual attentions of the new Cadet and Roxane. He signals
    this to Valvert.Then)*

VALVERT *(calling to Christian)*: The show is not up here,
                        boy! Turn your gaze some other place.

CHRISTIAN *(to himself)*: Were he down here,
                        I'd swiftly plant my glove upon his face.
    *(He reflexively reaches into his pocket for his glove
    and catches the Cut-Purse already there.)* I was seeking
    my glove.

CUT-PURSE *(cringing)*:   And instead found my hand.

CHRISTIAN: You had better explain this well.

CUT-PURSE: As you command.
    You see, uh, Valvert's quite the master of the sword.
        I intended to stop you before your blood poured
            o'er the floor.

CHRISTIAN: Your concern is most touching, but it will not do.
        I suggest you try again, villain, before *I* run *you* through.

CUT-PURSE: Better you should let me go.
    If so, I'll share a secret you might care to know.

CHRISTIAN: Go on.

CUT-PURSE: That friend of yours who just absconded –

CHRISTIAN: Ragueneau?

CUT-PURSE: He is done for. Kaput. Dead and gone.

CHRISTIAN *(releasing the rascal)*: How so?

CADET 1 *(striking once more)*:   Again, a hit!

CADET 2:   And now, that's it - I quit!

    *(Cadet 1 bows. 2 swats him on the hat with
    his foil. 1 chases 2 back to the other two Cadets.)*

CUT-PURSE: A song that he penned has angered
    (- he glances surreptitiously towards de Guiche -)
                            ...well, that is of no matter.
    But now one hundred men have been hired
                            to make his "ink" splatter –
    his "red" ink, you see?

CHRISTIAN: I understand. And the plan?

CUT-PURSE: Each comes brandishing –

CADET 3: *(oblivious to the above,*
    triumphantly announcing his card): A club!

CADET 4 *(trumping him)*:   A spade!

CUT-PURSE: a sword or a knife,
    to shred Ragueneau's cook book of life.

CHRISTIAN: For this, *one hundred* were paid?!

CUT-PURSE: Handsomely.

CHRISTIAN: And how is it you know that such plans were laid?

CUT-PURSE: Very simple.
                    One of the hundred – is me, I'm afraid.

CHRISTIAN: Engaged by whom?

CUT-PURSE *(another furtive glance at de Guiche)*: That I
                                cannot say. My apologies.
            After all, we do have our professional…courtesies.

CHRISTIAN: The ambush then. Where will you wait?

CUT-PURSE: Porte Saint-Denis. Just inside the gate.
        There is still time to inform Ragueneau before it is too late.
                …Not that it's any of my concern,
            but it's best you warn him not to return
        home tonight.

CHRISTIAN: But where to find him?

CUT-PURSE: That can't be too hard to discern.

CHRISTIAN *(calling)*: Citizens! If you please,
which is Ragueneau's *favorite* tavern?!

BELLEROSE *(busy eating his baked goods)*: Any within
lips' reach.

CADET 1: You might try the Notre Dram

CADET 2: or Sacre-Couer's Light.

CADET 3: The Mouthful.

CADET 4: The Eiffel.

BELLEROSE *(finding a special treat
in Ragueneau's container)*: Ooh, a candied yam!

MUSICIAN 1: The Horn of Plenty.

MUSICIAN 2: The Fiddle-De-Dee.

ORANGE GIRL: I believe it to be The Sans Souci.

MUSKETEER 1 *(looking at the
Orange Girl's chest)*: The Juicy Pear.
(All look at him.) I've seen him there!

LE BRET *(returning)*: No, de Neuvillette,
it is The Belt That Burst.

CUT-PURSE: Best leave a note at each. He has quite the thirst.

CHRISTIAN: I'll go, as I must. And on the run.
            To think, a hundred against just one!
(Looking longingly at Roxane) Oh,
  but to leave…her *(- and with an altogether different*
    glance at de Guiche and Valvert) with *them* - leaves me cold.
                        Still, unlucky Ragueneau must be told.

(Christian rushes to exit and collides with the entering Mus-
keteer 2.)

MUSKETEER 2: Whoa! Slow down, young man. Is there a fire?

CHRISTIAN: Pardon me, sir. Friendship does require
  that I fast depart, although in my heart
  I would stay to keep an eye on a certain Comte with ill intents.

MUSKETEER 2: Ah, de Guiche. Yes, I would think it hard
  to take one's eyes off a man so well-adorned in his
                                        accomplishments.
        (They bow to each other. Christian exits hurriedly. The
  Musketeer calls to de Guiche.) Beautiful ribbons, Comte!
            What is their color –

                        "Belly of the Doe?"

DE GUICHE: No, monsieur. I call this particular shade
                        "Fallen Spanish Foe."

MUSKETEER 2: Ha! Well said.
                Of our true colors let that be first of all,
    and before long, in Flanders, let us see the Spaniards fall.

DE GUICHE: We shall soon enough, good sir.
                But right now – the theater!
Bellerose! On your toes!
            I'm growing impatient. Let the play begin!

BELLEROSE *(bowing)*: Yes, Monsieur.

CADETS: Clear the floor!

(They put their "toys" away and turn their attentions to the stage within the stage.)

LE BRET *(purchasing a treat from the Orange Girl)*: Yes, let us see if Montfleury is in.

BELLEROSE *(to Musketeer 2)*: The fee, sir.

MUSKETEER 2 *(holding up a bill)*: Have you change?

BELLEROSE: Why, of course.
(But he can't find his purse.) Now, that's strange.

(He exits through the curtain, anxiously.)

ORANGE GIRL *(responding to Le Bret)*: Oh, but Captain, the actor does not dare.

LE BRET: Yet I don't see Cyrano anywhere.

(Bellerose re-enters through the curtain and bangs the traditional three knocks on the floor with his staff.There is a great hush.)

BELLEROSE: Monsieurs et Madames, in this Hall oh so hallow, we present "La Clorise" by Balthasar Baro. If you should like what you see-

CADETS 1 & 2: Get off the stage!

CADETS 3 & 4:   Montfleury!

(More hoots. Bellerose is soon shouted off the stage with other such cries demanding "Montfleury!" Some of the fruit bought from the Orange Girl makes its way in his direction. As he disappears there is great applause and the Musicians begin to play. The curtains part revealing a pastoral land-scape, its backdrop a moving panorama of rolling clouds and perhaps a rising sun run by the creaky stage machinery of the 17th century stage. Montfleury makes a grand entrance, a huge man whose bulk is accentuated by the absurdity of his costume – a rustic Arcadian shepherd's smock and a hat gar-landed with roses tilted over one ear. He is blowing on a pan pipe, his face heavily painted. The crowd cheers as the actor pompously – and repeatedly – bows, half-heartedly attempt-ing to stop the applause, an "offense to his modesty." He fi-nally begins, speaking the role of Phadon, the whole while casting a seductive gaze at Roxane, his lines a repugnant flir-tation.)

MONTFLEURY: "Thrice happy he who hides
                    from pomp and power
          In sylvan shade or solitary bower,
                    Where balmy zephyrs fan his burning cheeks – "

A VOICE *(from the recesses of the upper box,
     house left)*: Wretch! *(Music and scenery halt.)*
                              Did I not banish you a full three weeks?!

(Murmurs. Everyone looks about.)

MONTFLEURY: Oh, my dear sweet Mother!

ORANGE GIRL: Cyrano!

LE BRET: None other.

The VOICE: Exit post haste,
　　　you bombastic scene-chewing clown. Off the stage!

DE GUICHE: What nonsense!
　　　Montfleury, you need not put up with this outrage.

MONTFLEURY:　　　No, of course. It will not do.
　　(To the Voice) Tell me, Monsieur, where are you?

The VOICE: Here and *hear*ing!　Displeased as I am disobeyed.

(More murmurs.)

DE GUICHE: Silence!　　Go on, Montfleury. Do not be afraid.

MONTFLEURY *(with far less confidence, nodding for
　　the musicians to resume their play, signaling the
　　scenery to roll)*: Ahem. "Thrice happy he who hides from - "

The VOICE: Me!　*(Sound and scenery again
　　　grind to a halt.)*　Be advised you had best play mum.
　If you dare breathe one balmy zephyr more,
　　I will fan *your* cheeks until they are gore.

(Montfleury turns on his heels.)

DE GUICHE: Hold, Montfleury!　The show will go on.

MONTFLEURY:　　Yes, and Jodelet can play Phadon!

The VOICE:　A good idea, Windbag, for if you *were* to dare,
　　　I'd have to puncture you!　...And let out the hot air.

(Murmurs, laughs.)

DE GUICHE: Who owns this insolent voice?
   My annoyance with it grows.

BELLEROSE: It's that of Cyrano, sir, de Bergerac,
                          who'd have our "Clorise" close.

DE GUICHE: Well, where is the scoundrel? Where is he?
Can anybody tell me that? Where, Valvert?
        (He shakes his head.) Where, Bellerose?
          (The same response.) Where, Montfleury?

VALVERT, BELLEROSE & MONTFLEURY: Who
"KNOWS?"

CYRANO *(leaning so far forward*
                he is practically out of the box): *"NOSE?!"*
   *(There is a moment of dead silence. Then Cyrano
     continues with great calm.)*
                          Before I lose all patience, Montfleury – flee.
                          I'm less a pretty sight when I grow angry.
   *(There are loud murmurs of dissent from de Guiche,
    Valvert, Bellerose and the musicians.)* Protests?! *(The
    crowd quiets again as Cyrano casually sits himself on the
    railing of the box.)* Then I hereby issue a challenge to one and all
       who would fight to see this poseur desecrate this sacred hall.
   Le Bret! Begin a list of those who would keep him in the cast.
     (To audience) Come, give us your names,
                       you who would be the first to breathe their last.
                            Hmm? You? You? You? You? You?
   *(- Each "You" spoken while pointing his sword at Bellerose,
    the musicians, and several audience members.)* Ah,
                                         Montfleury – adieu.
      Oh, but wait! It may only be that they misunderstand.
       (To audience again) To simplify:
                       Whoever wants to die, please raise your hand.

(No takers. With a shrug to Le Bret)
          Perhaps a naked sword offends their modesty?

(He tosses his unsheathed sword to Le Bret.)

LE BRET: Maybe so, Cyrano.

CYRANO: All right then, where were we?
  Ah, yes! *(He makes a particularly acrobatic entrance*
  from the upper box onto the stage. Montfleury flinches.)
               I want this swollen carbuncle excised,
  and this *(taking his sword back)* shall serve
                  as my scalpel extemporized.

MONTFLEURY *(his back against the wall)*: Sir,
        when you threaten me, you offend the Muse!

CYRANO: What is offensive is the way you abuse
  this grand artistic calling.
   Your acting is appalling.
               All that "mincing" and "indicating"
             has me wincing! It's irritating
  to see a stage so poorly used.
 The Muse would not be a*mused*!

DE GUICHE: Montfleury, I assure you wholeheartedly,
            you need pay no attention to this heckler.
  De Valvert, go down to the floor,
         and show that interloper to the door.

MONTFLEURY *(bowing)*:   My protector.

(Valvert exits the box. Cyrano paces the staged
displeased.)

DE GUICHE: Bellerose! Resume.

(Bellerose signals the musicians to begin yet again. The scenery cranks. Montfleury screws up his courage, his eyes now only on Cyrano.)

MONTFLEURY *(soft and high-pitched,
                    with a catch in his throat)*: "Thrice hap-"

CYRANO *(turning on him)*: "Hap-hap-hap!" *Thrice* will I clap!

(Music and scenery grind to a halt one last time.)

MONTFLEURY *(shaking in his slippers)*: ...Clap?!

CYRANO: Yes, clap; and upon my third,
                    not a further word best pass through those lips.
         Instead, Montfleury,
      you will make like the round moon that you are – and eclipse!

MUSKETEER 1: He'll stay.

MUSKETEER 2:   He'll go.

MUSKETEER 1: You think?

MUSKETEER 2:   I know.

MONTFLEURY: Sir –

CYRANO: Thrice!
                    And thrice only, you half-baked ham. I say: Thrice!
         Then if you are not gone, *I* shall remove you –
(with a punctuating flourish or two of his sword) slice by slice!

MONTFLEURY: But – but –

CYRANO *(clapping)*:   One.

MONTFLEURY: See here –

CYRANO *(clapping)*: Two. *(As Cyrano opens his
    hands for a third clap, Montfleury disappears
    screaming, perhaps knocking down a good bit of
    scenery on his way. Cyrano claps a third time.)*   Three.

CADETS: Au revoir, Montfleury!

(They cheer.)

CYRANO *(to de Guiche)*:   "La comedie est fini."

DE GUICHE *(to Roxane)*:   Mademoiselle. Follow me.

*(They exit the box, Roxane grabbing her Duenna's hand on
the way.)*

BELLEROSE: Come, Cyrano,
    what reasons have you to hate Montfleury as you do?

CYRANO: My dear Monsieur Le Directeur Bellerose,
                        I have exactly two.
The first of which, I do believe, I may have previously suggested:
    Lines cultivated to feed the soul,
                        spew out of him but half-digested.

BELLEROSE: Hmpf! And the second?

CYRANO: Ah, I do regret,
        Bellerose, that's to remain… my secret.

MUSICIAN 1:   But, sir, you rob us of "Clorise,"

MUSICIAN 2: Baro's eternal masterpiece.

BELLEROSE: Surely we don't deserve this!

CYRANO: The poetry of Baro being what it is,
                    you should consider this a public service.

CUT-PURSE: Nevertheless, de Bergerac,
          we (- *gesturing to the audience*) will want our money back.

MUSICIAN 1:   And our salaries!

MUSICIAN 2: In *full*, if you please.

  (Bellerose's knees buckle. He is caught by Le Bret.)

MUSICIAN 2: We're artists. We don't compromise,

MUSICIAN 1:   especially not on the size...

BOTH MUSICIANS: ...of our purses!

BELLEROSE: A thousand curses!

CYRANO: There now, take comfort, Bellerose.
                    I shall allay all of your woes.
                              (Tossing Bellerose his purse) Catch!

BELLEROSE *(weighing the purse in his hand and reviving
    immediately)*: My dear sir, on these terms,
you have my permission to close the theater any time you choose.

CYRANO *(to audience)*: Individual - as well as mercantile –
                    support is a resource the arts must never lose.

BELLEROSE *(bowing to Cyrano,*
    then addressing the audience): Madames et Monsieurs,
                    all refunds will be made to the very last sou.
We ask only that you remain in your seats until I form a queue.
        (Shouting to his company) Actors, tear her down! Jodelet
                    lower the lights!

VOICE OF JODELET: First, *raise* my pay!

BELLEROSE: Laggard, you're lucky to get –

(The chandelier drops, nearly killing him.)

VOICE OF JODELET: Sorry. Just striking the set.

*(Bellerose gestures wildly to the Musicians to finish striking
the production before exiting the house. The Cut-Purse follows, no more than a few steps behind, his eyes glued to that
purse. As they go, de Valvert steps out of the shadows of the
stage. [The "strike" should consist of lowering the second
chandelier, though not extinguishing either of them, perhaps
removing the two benches, and whatever else will facilitate
the coming scene change.])*

VALVERT: Montfleury, gone. The Great Montfleury.
                    You, monsieur, have caused quite the scandal.

CYRANO *(bowing)*: Thank you, sir. I do my best.
                    But rest assured; it's nothing I can't handle.

VALVERT: Did you know he has a powerful patron?

CYRANO: Indeed! Well, were you aware that I have none?

VALVERT: And this patron's arm is rather long.
                              It reaches right to the Bastille.

CYRANO: Yet mine may be even longer yet, sir
        (- *his hand on his sword*) – by a good three feet of steel.

DE GUICHE (*entering the scene, followed by Roxane
    and her Duenna*): Sadly, your manners –
                    and taste in art - reflect a culture in decline.

CYRANO: Rather it is you, Monsieur Le Comte,
                    whom I would call the Philistine.

LE BRET (*warning his friend*): Cyrano.

DE GUICHE: And I presume you find yourself a Samson.
                                    Is that so?

CYRANO: Well, you know,
            I need only the jawbone of an *ass*, and I can show
    that to be true. Perhaps you'll lend me yours?

LE BRET: Cyrano, take care!

CYRANO: Bah!

LE BRET: Oh, zut alors!

DE GUICHE (*to Le Bret*): Your friend grows tiresome.
            (*To no one in particular*) Will no one end this tedium?

VALVERT (*looking at the audience*): No one?

Than *I* shall do it, using his own medium
 – words. *(He approaches Cyrano slowly.*
The two men size each other up.) Ah, yes...your nose.
...Your nose... It...is...is...

CYRANO: Divine?!
              Sir, know that I do glory in this nose of mine.
    For a great nose indicates
       a great *(- touching his head -)* mind,
     large *(- touching his chest -)* heart,
  and big *(- he reaches toward his crotch) -*

ORANGE GIRL: Monsieur!

CYRANO *(completing his interrupted gesture,*
                       pointing to his boots): - feet.
   Which, on my word, I would happily apply directly to your seat
       if only I could tell it from your face -
           one so entirely devoid of grace,
                          of pride, of poetry and/or of prose,
                       of character – in short – devoid of... *Nose.*

VALVERT: Ahem. As I was saying, your nose is...rather...

CYRANO: Yes?

VALVERT: Big!

   (A collective gasp. Then utter silence. Cyrano signals
   that there is no cause for alarm. Yet.)

CYRANO *(gravely)*: Ah!

VALVERT: Ha!

CYRANO: Is that the best you can do?

VALVERT: What?

CYRANO: There are so many more eloquent options;
                    allow me to provide you with but a few
    on the subject you chose to broach.
    For example – There's the *Approach*…

    Aggressive: That nose is a disgrace.
                    I'd cut it off to please, not spite, my face.
    Descriptive: 'Tis a rock – a peak – a cape. Aha,
                    I have it now! It's rather a penisula!
    Curious: Forgive me, I just need to know.
                    Is that a pencil box or a portfolio?
Kind: That you love the little birds can be swiftly deduced
    by the perch you provide upon which all of them can roost.
Insolent: Sir, when you smoke the situation must seem dire
                    As your neighbors rush about screaming:
                                    "Your chimney is on fire!"

LE BRET: *Academic*!

CYRANO: *Academic*: One mathematical treasure –
    A factual proboscis *beyond* all means of measure.
                              We can only estimate its size
                              as no arithmetic law applies.
    (Applause. Then to Valvert) Care for another? Men?

CADET 1:   Um…*Cosmopolitan*!

CYRANO: Fashionable *and* functional that.
    The quite perfect hook to hang your hat.

CADET 2: *Rustic*!

CYRANO: *Rustic*: Call that a nose?
   Looks to me like a garden hose.
    Geographical: Is that China's Great Wall
                      or the Pyramid at Giza?
   No, no; whatever could I be thinking? -
                    It's the Leaning Tower of Pisa!

CADETS 3 & 4: *Emphatic*!

CYRANO: Beware your sneeze –
          a blowing hurricane breeze!

(Cadets 3 and 4 twirl toward him as if blown by a wind.)

BELLEROSE: *Dramatic*.

CYRANO: My brothers, when it bleeds – the Red Sea.

*(Cadets 3 and 4 hold their hats beneath his
nose as buckets.)*

CUT-PURSE: *Enterprising*!

CYRANO: A sign for a perfumery!

(Cadets 3 and 4 retreat, holding their noses.)

MUSKETEER 2: Try *Beastiary*!

CYRANO: At least a theory:
   To the pachyderm you must be related,
for your own trunk, sir, is no less "truncated."

BOTH MUSICIANS: *Lyric*!

CYRANO: Is this the conch that Triton blew?

ORANGE GIRL: *Naive*!

CYRANO: When is the monument on view?
 Oh, but Vicomte de Valvert, we've yet to hear from you.

VALVERT (*at a loss*):   Why, this is crazy.

CYRANO: Come now, you're just being lazy.

VALVERT (*insulted*): Lazy?!

CYRANO: "Lazy" it is!
            (*Condescendingly to Valvert*) Well done. - *Lazy*:
   Why not take the easy way out,
   and wear that elongated snout wrapped 'round your shoulder?
   Do I nonplus you? Here's *Industrious*, too:
            Best make that old grind*stone*...a boulder.
 (*To all*) Quick, another!

LE BRET: Holy Mother...?
 ...Ah, *Classical*!

CYRANO: Sir, you have a Roman nose.
                    It's "Roman" all over your face!

ALL CADETS (*with a sharp salute*): *Military*!

CYRANO: Forward march, Gascon Cadets!
        (*They join him.*) We shall capture it for our base.

DUENNA: *Tasteless*, sir.

CYRANO: Does it smell!

(For the first time, there is absolutely no reaction.)
                                    It's "*s*not" funny? Ah, well.

MUSKETEER 1: *Tasty.*

CYRANO: Are you going to eat that banana or just wear it?

ROXANE *(applauding)*: Encore!

CYRANO *(bowing)*: One more, if that be your wish

ROXANE: Oh yes, I so declare it.

CYRANO: *Shakespearean*
    (spoken with a touch of melancholy): An "*infinite*" jest.
  (To Valvert) Well, there you are, sir. Please be my guest.
    Feel free to tuck away any quip that I've said.
Take several, for surely there's room in your head
    for many.

VALVERT: What?

CYRANO: Well, Vicomte, I would submit,
  you do not have one speck of original wit.
    In fact, "wit" is a word I doubt you can spell,
    which, come to think of it, may be just as well,
          for while I mock my own self now and for ever,
              do I let another try? No, monsieur. Never!
      Luckily, as a man of *letters* you are no success,
  unless, of course, you were to count the letters a-s-s.

VALVERT *(raging)*:   Such ludicrous grand airs!

DE GUICHE *(trying to lead Valvert away)*: Vicomte, come.

VALVERT *(breaking away)*:   How he dares
to speak this way to me, when look at him. His colors – bland!
  No ribbons, lace, or buckled shoes. Not even gloves in hand!
    (To Cyrano) Just who do you think you are,
                                   you ill-bred uncivilized hack!?

CYRANO *(removing his hat, bowing deeply)*: I am
                    Cyrano – Savinien – Hercule – de – Bergerac.
    (And aside to de Guiche) Will he remember half of that?
                         (Back to Valvert)…At your service.

LE BRET: Friend Cyrano, your comportment makes me nervous.
  Let this be.

CYRANO *(waving his friend off)*: It's true,
                    I don no foppish rigmarole.
  I choose instead to wear *my* adornments on my soul.
   A simple plume shows spirit. But a peacock's tail - absurd!
      I care not at all for such frills, but rather deed and word,
                and twirl my pointed wit like a mustache.
                You see, what *suits* me best is my panache.
            …But then you mentioned gloves. You have me there.
                         I do have an old one, left from a pair.
      But of the other, there is not a trace.
  You see, I left it in some Vicomte's face.

VALVERT *(incensed)*:   Why, you insolent pup!

  (Cyrano howls like a dog and then doubles over moaning.)

CYRANO: Oh, how it stiffens up!

VALVERT *(to de Guiche)*: Now what?

CYRANO: Ooh! Oww! I need relieve this cramp so deep.
            From lack of exercise, my sword has gone to sleep.

*(Laughter. Cyrano acknowledges the praise for
his performance.)*

VALVERT: Well, perhaps this will wake it!

*(He smacks his glove across Cyrano's face. There is
utter silence as Cyrano fingers his offended nose.)*

CYRANO *(quietly)*:   Good thing you didn't break it
   for this thing might swell to such extents
            It would smother half the audience.

VALVERT *(drawing his sword; contemptuously)*: Poet.

CYRANO: If you will.
                  So shall I compose you a Ballade as we fence,
proving, once and for all, the compatibility of swords and pens?

VALVERT: A Ballade?

CYRANO: Yes, Ballade – a verse of rather rigid form.
   You are familiar, of course, with its customary norm:
            Three eight-line stanzas followed by a refrain of four.
                  Oh, and at the end of its lines…I settle our score!

VALVERT: Will you?

CYRANO: I will. *(Then quieting his foe with a gesture)*
            "Ballade of the Duel at the Hotel de Bourgogne This Day
      Between Cyrano de Bergerac and a Contemptible Popinjay."

VALVERT: Good. Now are you done with your little "recital?"

CYRANO: My dear Vicomte, that was only the title.

(The crowd laughs.)

MUSKETEER 2: All right, citizens –

MUSKETEER 1:   Stand clear!

DE GUICHE: Be careful not to interfere.

CADETS 1 & 2: Let's give them room!

CADETS 3 & 4:   Move back!

LE BRET: Come on, Cadets – Bivouac!

DUENNA *(as Musketeer 1 draws uncomfortably
            close to her)*: You sir! Don't even try it!

BELLEROSE: Would everyone please be quiet!

*(The onlookers are now in fine viewing positions.
Valvert stands poised, weapon in hand. But Cyrano, sword
not yet drawn, is still, his eyes closed. Valvert indicates his
perplexity to de Guiche who only shrugs in reply.)*

VALVERT: Frightened, de Bergerac?
                    Are you praying for a miracle?

CYRANO: No, searching for something lyrical.
                    …Ah! I have it, and in full!

*(In the duel that follows, Cyrano's actions should match his
words. He clears his throat, and signals the musicians for
some accompaniment to underscore his Ballade.)*

With grace, I toss away my hat,
   (- to the Orange Girl)
Then drape this cloak so very "bland"
Upon my waiting arm – like that.
Drawing my sword, held high in hand,
Like Scaramouche, I rend the sky!
Thus, Vicomte, in this 'pointed' way
My honor I shall satisfy
When at the refrain's end – touché.

Now where to skewer my peacock,
To clip his wings and watch him crawl?
The crest? The breast? Or even sock?
Ah, Groin! No, *that* target's far too small.
To find a spot 'twixt bow and lace
One might well study for a day!
I'll strive here for a faster pace,
And at the refrain's end – touché

I need a rhyme for one more verse,
While you need end your sad travails.
Will your flailing courage disperse
Before my keen invention fails?
Your thrust is weak, parried with ease.
Your vision blurs. Your feet are clay.
But it's much too late to appease
For at the refrain's end – Touché.

(He solemnly announces)

REFRAIN: *(The music stops.)*
Vicomte, pray pardon from on High
For your provoking this meleé.
I lunge, I feint – and wave goodbye
At this, the refrain's end -

(He knocks the sword out of Valvert's hand.)

   Touché!

*(He pokes his opponent in the nose – with his nose!
Valvert falls in a sitting position.)*

The CROWD: Bravo! Bravo! Bravo!

CYRANO *(sheathing his sword)*:   And better than Baro.

*(Enraged, Valvert finds his sword and attacks Cyrano behind
his back.)*

LE BRET: Cyrano!

CYRANO *(after deftly fending off the lunge)*:
                    Behind my back, Vicomte?
                         Why, I would have thought you better bred.
If it is not too late to learn, you had best quit before certain –

VALVERT: Bloodshed?
    Yes, yours, de Bergerac, for I shan't quit until you're dead.

*(He lunges. The two duel furiously. Finally, de Bergerac
disarms his opponent who drops to his knees.)*

CYRANO *(to others)*: I wonder; will losing a nose
                         teach one to keep his head?

*(Cyrano coolly slices Valvert's nose open. There is a collec-
tive gasp as he does so. The Musicians attend to the fallen
duelist now clutching his nose with both hands. A Musketeer
breaks through the crowd and approaches Cyrano as the*

*others jabber to one another about the combat before gradu-
ally resuming their business.)*

MUSKETEER 2 *(with outstretched hand)*: Ah, monsieur,
                    if you will permit me saying so, most well done!
              I have a certain appreciation for this sort of fun,
and heartily salute your handiness, your audacity, and your brio.

   (He salutes and exits.)

CYRANO *(to Le Bret)*: Who was that?

LE BRET: Oh…D'Artagnan. Used to cavort with that
                                        Musketeer trio.
   (Cyrano still can't quite place him.) Oh, you know,
that "All for one, and *free* for all!" Lots of bluster and bravado.

CYRANO: Yes, but remind me to catch up with him.
                    I think I can improve that motto.

ROXANE *(pulling him aside, with some urgency)*: Cyrano.

CYRANO: Sweet cousin.

ROXANE: Thank you so.

CYRANO: My dear Roxane, thank me for what I'd like to know.

ROXANE: Oh, say for your panache.

DE GUICHE *(calling)*: Roxane!

ROXANE *(to Cyrano)*: But I must dash.

*(She exchanges a brief look with Cyrano, and goes
to de Guiche who makes his farewell to Cyrano.)*

DE GUICHE: We shall meet again.

CYRANO: Ah, but who "*knows*" (- *tapping his nose*) when?

*(He bows. De Guiche returns the gesture and exits
along with the two Musicians and Bellerose, supporting
Valvert. Roxane and the Duenna follow. Just as the Duenna
is about to exit, Musketeer 1 grabs her hand, draws her back,
and plants a kiss. She either slaps him in the face or pushes
him down before completing her exit. He recovers, smiles
broadly – he likes them feisty – and pursues her off with a
spring in his step.)*

LE BRET *(helping Cyrano on with his cloak)*: Not, I hope,
     until after you join me for some dinner. We need to talk.

CYRANO: No dining for me;
     I seem hell-bent on growing thinner. But shall we walk?

LE BRET: What's this? I've never known a fight
                         not to whet your appetite.
The very idea of you passing up a meal is a notion I find funny.

CYRANO: Oh, my hunger is quite intact, my dear old friend.
   What I lack, you see, is
                    (- *making certain the Cadets can't hear* -) money.

LE BRET *(while miming a toss)*: But that purse of gold
   you gave away?

CYRANO: Farewell, paternal pension!

LE BRET: So, you have until next month exactly what?

CYRANO: Do I need mention?
    (Making a "goose-egg" with his hand
    around his nose) Zero.

LE BRET: A stupid act!

CYRANO: But a glorious gesture!

LE BRET: Zero?!

CYRANO: Zero!

    (The Orange Girl, while approaching to return Cyrano's hat,
    has overheard everything.)

ORANGE GIRL *(handing Cyrano his hat, timidly)*: Pardon,
             sir. One ought never go hungry, especially a hero.
    If you please. *(Displaying her wares)*
                        Help yourself to all that you see.

CYRANO: Le Bret, have you ever known such charity?
        Dear sweet child, my Gascon pride, you must understand,
             forbids my taking anything – except your hand.

    (He takes it and, his nose in the way, kisses it with
    some awkwardness.)

ORANGE GIRL: Thank you, monsieur. *(Offering the food*
    again) But won't you –

    (Cyrano stops her with a gesture of his hand. She curtsies
    and crosses away just as Montfleury tries to sneak back on
    stage. One of the Cadets notices him.)

CADET 1: Hey, boys, do you see what I see?

CADET 4: He's hard to miss.

ALL CADETS: Oh, Montfleury!

*(He looks towards them, they raise their swords, and he
bolts off stage, the Cadets in joyful pursuit, crossing paths
with the re-entering Musicians who are spun about first
by the fleeing actor and then repeatedly by the Cadets.)*

CYRANO: So you wished to talk, Le Bret?

LE BRET: Yes. Tell me,
  just how do you think your "escapades" are met?
    And why must you unceasingly offend
  all those on who your future may depend?

CYRANO: I have acquired some new foes, you are afraid?

LE BRET: Ha!

CYRANO: How many today would you guess I've made?

LE BRET *(dismissing this
  as ridiculous)*: Far too many to calibrate!

CYRANO: But surely you can estimate?!

CUT-PURSE *(exiting)*: There's de Guiche.

MUSICIANS 1 & 2: The Vicomte de Valvert.

CYRANO: Music to my ears!

ORANGE GIRL: Baro.

LE BRET: Montfleury,
and *(gesturing toward the audience)*
quite possibly every single last member of the Academy!

CYRANO: Bliss!

LE BRET: The man's impossible!
  (To Cyrano) Why is it you seem to relish each new enemy?

CYRANO: Because I do!
            As a cure for ennui, and a mark of my identity –
    as notable as *(indicating his nose) this*! Know,
                  Le Bret, that I choose each foe
            with the same care and vigilance as a friend,
              expecting both to be with me to the end.

LE BRET: That is, until you are dead.

CYRANO: Smack! You've hit it on the head!

LE BRET: Hmmph! Well then,
  what's the real reason you've made Montfleury your foe?
  Come, Cyrano, reveal the secret. Why do you hate him so?

CYRANO: That histrionic bellowing belly
    dreams that he turns women into jelly.

LE BRET: And so what is that to you?

CYRANO: My friend, not a drop of dew…
  until I witnessed his eyes pursue
    my precious, dearest…

LE BRET: Some ingenue?

CYRANO: Would it not make your nature sour
              to see a slug crawl o'er a flower?

LE BRET *(amazed)*: Is it possible?

CYRANO *(pulling him far downstage)*: For me to love? …I love.

LE BRET: Well, that's one subject you've never spoken of.
    …I never knew.
      May I ask who?

CYRANO: Think a moment.
          Think of me – the most unlikely lover in all of France,
    with a nose that announces my presence
                              a good full hour in advance.
Of course, in the mocking way of the world, I would be fated
              to love the loveliest woman that God ever created.
    Most sweet, most wise, most witty, and most fair.

LE BRET: Who is this woman so beyond compare?

CYRANO: Who? *She.* Dangerous, mortally, without meaning.
                  Exquisite beyond imagination's gleaning.
    Oh, to know her smile is to know a perfect thing.
She who with one small turn of her head does bring
          heaven to earth, making life worth living…even dear.

LE BRET *(facetiously)*: Well, of course,
                  that makes everything perfectly clear!
    (Pause.) Wait a minute; it's your cousin –
      Madeleine Robin!

CYRANO: Yes, Roxane.

LE BRET: Then if you love her, why not tell her so?

CYRANO: Ha-Ha! A brilliant plan!

LE BRET: Well, it was rather quite evident tonight,
        you covered yourself with glory in her sight.

CYRANO: My old friend, look at me. Tell me what chance
                    I really have with this protuberance!
    No, I have no illusions.
        Oh, sometimes on an evening's stroll, my heart will sing
    as this preposterous appendage
                    breathes in the hope and promise of the Spring.
    Then, embraced by the moon's resplendent silver light,
        I dream of walking arm in arm into the night.
            Yes, I dream – and I forget. Then my damned eyes fall
                on my profile's shadow, moon-cast upon a wall.

LE BRET: Dear Cyrano.

CYRANO: Bitter days I have known
    finding myself so ugly, and alone.
        Sometimes…

LE BRET: You weep?

CYRANO: Never that!
        I'll not so profane the dignity of sorrow
    to have a tear trickle down this slope
                and not reach bottom 'til tomorrow.
I would not turn something so sublime as tears to the ridiculous.

LE BRET: My old friend, I tell you –
                    you have no good cause to be unhappy thus.
Why, that poor child, who just now offered you a meal,

whose hand you tickled with a kiss, one could not steal
                    her eyes away from you – not even for a bit.

CYRANO: That's true.

LE BRET: Well then! Where is your courage and your wit?
  Roxane herself, watching your fight,
     turned as pale as cold moon light.

CYRANO: Did she?

LE BRET *(dramatically)*: Her hand thus, at her breast,
          her lips parted,...*(dismissively)* and all the rest.
     Go speak to her, man! Speak to her, and she will hear.

CYRANO: Or laugh at me, the one thing in the world I fear.

   *(Roxane's Duenna enters with a note
   and makes a sweeping curtsey.)*

DUENNA: Monsieur. If you please.

CYRANO *(to Le Bret)*: Le Bret, it's *her* Duenna!

LE BRET *(grabbing the note
                    and passing it to Cyrano)*: Yes, with a delivery.

CYRANO *(scrutinizing the message)*: Roxane desires
  that we meet!

LE BRET *(slapping an arm around his friend)*: Us?
  How nice.

CYRANO: No! She and I!

DUENNA: In privacy!
  (Le Bret backs off.)
  ...although for the very life of me I can't imagine why
  or –

LE BRET *(cutting her off)*: When?

CYRANO *(reading)*: "Tomorrow, after Mass,
                    as the break of day draws nigh."

DUENNA: You sir, are to choose a spot
                    where no one can dare eavesdrop.

CYRANO *(too nervous to think straight)*: Mon dieu!
  Oh, where, Le Bret?! Where?!

LE BRET: Where else?

CYRANO: Ragueneau's bake shop!

DUENNA *(with another bow)*: My mistress will be there
                                    sharply at seven.

  (Exits.)

CYRANO: And I am bound straightaway to heaven!

LE BRET: Well, do come back before morning
                    or you'll miss you-know-who.

CYRANO: Le Bret – my dearest, oldest friend –
                          I have a rendezvous!

LE BRET: Why not call it a tryst?

CYRANO: Roxane knows I exist!!!

LE BRET: I'm pleased for you. So now you can relax.

CYRANO: Relax?! When, suddenly, my heart attacks
  my very reason? No, I must rally to its cause,
                                    follow it into the fray
and prove without delay that I am –

LE BRET: – once again, as usual, carried away?

CYRANO: Oh, Le Bret.
      Today – right now – I want whole armies to oppose!
I have ten hearts, twenty arms, and *one enormous NOSE*
      that I will blow like a trumpet to the last!
I cannot be contained; bring me something vast!

  *(Ragueneau enters, staggering drunk, weeping profusely,
  a half-dozen or more pieces of paper clenched in his
  hand.)*

RAGUENEAU *(slurring his words)*: Death! Doom!
                                    Apotheosis of catastrophes!

CYRANO: Ragueneau, what's wrong?

RAGUENEAU *(in his drunken panic,
  unable to articulate, but delighted to see Cyrano)*: You! –
                      They – I – Aah - ...Here, read these.

CYRANO *(reading from Christian's
  tavern messages)*: …"Cut-throats"…"Porte Saint-Denis"…

RAGUENEAU: Goodbye, world! Woe is me!

CYRANO *(smiling broadly)*: 　　… "a full one hundred strong!"

RAGUENEAU: 　　　　　　　　　All this over a song!
　　Now I can't go home because of my fool pen.
　　(Crying) Never to see Lise, my poor widow, again!

CYRANO: Friend, you shall sleep soundly tonight
　　　　　　　　　　　　　　　in your very own bed;
fear not! *(And calling to offstage Cadets, who enter, and to the
　　others still onstage)*
　　　　　　　　Come as witnesses all to see these one hundred
fall. Take those candles for torches, but before we proceed
every Cadet must understand this: You shall not intercede.
(The Cadets grumble.) Hear me!
　(Silence.) No matter the threat, only *I* raise a sword.
Now, I need to know you agree. What say you?

CADETS *(disappointedly)* 　　　　　　　D'accord.

ORANGE GIRL *(as she and the Cadets remove candles
　　from the lowered chandeliers)*: But, monsieur,
　　　　　　　　　　　　one against a hundred men?

CYRANO: 　　　　　　Tonight I'd take a hundred more again!

*(The Orange Girl heaves a sigh, looks at her hand,
and then slaps Ragueneau with it, he having tried to
filch a drink from her.)*

LE BRET: But why risk your life for this fool howling drunk?

CYRANO: 　　Now, Le Bret, don't get into a growling funk.
There are two reasons.

LE BRET: 　Always "two!"

CYRANO: The first honors an act of grace
  that, some years ago, both touched my heart
                    and brought a smile onto my face:
    At Mass one Sunday,
      our poor Ragueneau spied the girl he later was to marry.

LE BRET: Lise.

CYRANO *(nodding)*: She dipped her fingers
          in the Holy Water, and our friend here did not tarry.
    He leapt the pews – who'd think him so spry? –
            bent down at the font, and drank it dry!

LE BRET: Charming. And the second?

CYRANO: Ah, Le Bret.
              How's it possible you could neglect
          this? If I fail to heed this warning,
    his shop won't open come the morning…

LE BRET & CYRANO *(simultaneously)*: And then
                    you/I would miss your/my rendezvous!

CYRANO *(to others)*:   Now come, all of you. Musicians too.
                Play as we march, your most rousing of tunes!

  *(They begin to play. Ragueneau is stirred
  and rises shakily.)*

RAGUENEAU: That's it, Cyrano! You lead and…

LE BRET *(as Ragueneau collapses)*:   …he swoons.

CYRANO: The advance begins. What will be, will be.

CADETS: To the Porte Saint-Denis! And Victory!

CYRANO *(to the Orange Girl)*: Did you not ask, child,
         why a hundred men are sent to threaten one poor poet?
    I shall tell you why.
         Because he is a friend of mine, and the villains know it!

*(The music swells as Cyrano draws his sword and
leads the raucous candlelit procession off. Ragueneau
reeling, cannot seem to find his way. Cyrano returns
and drags him off-stage.)*

Scene ii: The Poet's Patisserie.

*(The scene shift music changes, assuming a light and comic
tone, as three Baker Apprentices enter for a clown sequence
that completes the change into "Ragueneau's Patisserie" the
next morning. The front of the shop appears upstage – a wall
with a functional door topped by a hanging bell that rings
when it opens and closes. The street, seen vaguely through
the glass panes, is gray in the first light of dawn. Outsized
pastries, etc. are displayed in the "windows," each flagged
with a long descriptive poem. Humming or singing, each apprentice wheels in a castered table in a little choreographed
ballet. All of these tables are draped by cloths scribbled in
French text - more "poems" - covering what appear to be
mounds of baked goods. There is an inverted stool on each
table, as well. Through commedia-like "lazzi," the tables and
stools are placed, ending in a noisy commotion between the
apprentices. A voice interrupts the action and stops the music.)*

VOICE: Shh!

(The apprentices are perplexed and a little frightened. They attempt to locate the voice, going to the first draped table and, together, lifting its cloth. Magnificent pastries, cakes, rolls, and other such confections are revealed.)

ALL APPRENTICES *(ecstatic)*: Ooooooh!

(They proceed to the second, similarly unveiling more such scrumptious-looking treats.)

ALL APPRENTICES *(delighted)*:   Mmmmm!

(They go to the last table and lift its cloth, only to discover a hung-over Ragueneau who had been sleeping there.)

ALL APPRENTICES *(shocked)*:   Argggh!!!

RAGUENEAU *(rising, with some difficulty, empty bottle in hand)*: It's only me, the one who employs you, so if you please – *(raising his voice angrily)* a little less noise!
                                        (That hurt.) Ooh…

ALL APPRENTICES: Shh!

RAGUENEAU: All right, my apprentices;
                        let's see what you've baked today.

(They display their wares.)

APPRENTICE 1:   Marzipan!

APPRENTICE 2:   And this flan!

RAGUENEAU: Ah!

APPRENTICE 3:   Croquem-brouches! Croutes soufflé!

APPRENTICE 1: Beignet!

APPRENTICE 2:   *Bag*els!

APPRENTICE 3: And les Petit Fours avec frois Fruits en Gelée
    sous Bonbons Fondant de Brillot-Savarin a la Creme Glacés!

(Apprentice 3 reveals a donut-hole-sized ball of dough.)

APPRENTICE 1: Oh, but Master, I have saved the best for last!

(All head for Apprentice 1's table.)

RAGUENEAU: Stop right there, my apprentices! Not so fast!
        There's a question I've been meaning to ask you three,
                and you all must swear to answer it *honestly*!
    *(The apprentices react nervously as Ragueneau picks
    up two cherry-topped muffins that catch his eye.)*
    Have you seen anyone in this patisserie –
    Oh dear, how can I put this delicately? –
        play "pat–a-*cake*" –

ALL APPRENTICES: "Pat-a-cake?"

RAGUENEAU: Yes, you know – *(he absently "juggles" the
    muffins at chest-level, their cherry-tops facing front, making
    them look remarkably like pastry breasts)* "pat-a-cake!"
                                    …with my dear wife?

(All respond in turn with false incredulity.)

APPRENTICE 3: What, with Madame *Loose*?
    I mean – *LISE*!

APPRENTICE 2:   The very idea!

APPRENTICE 1 *(an oath)*:   Upon my life!
   You, master, a cuckold?

ALL APPRENTICES *(a little too emphatically)*:   Nooo!!!

RAGUENEAU *(his head hurting)*: Shh!
   (Still skeptical) Very well then. *(To Apprentice 1)* Come, show
                    me your new "pièce de résistance,"
   (and as 1 rushes to get it) though such adamant insistence
about my Lise makes me wonder if all you say is true.

APPRENTICE 1: Good Master Ragueneau,
                    if I might, you see before you
   nothing other than –

   *(1 reveals an elaborate confection, a pastry in the form
   of an ancient lyre, and Ragueneau totally forgets his
   suspicions.)*

RAGUENEAU *(unable to contain his awe)*:   - a *LYRE!*

APPRENTICE 2 & 3 *(whispering, having heard
   "Liar")*: We're caught!

APPRENTICE 2 *(still whispering)*:   Now Madame's to fire
                    us all for sure!

APPRENTICE 3 *(the same)*: But not before
                            cutting off our-

RAGUENEAU *(his woes all but forgotten
         as he examines the lyre)*: Whole wheat flour?

APPRENTICE 1: Master?

RAGUENEAU: In this poet's lyre?

APPRENTICES 2 & 3 (*greatly relieved,*
  collapsing in each other's arms): Phew!

APPRENTICE 1:   Oh no, sir, it's made entire-
                      ly of your incomparable almond paste,
  with barley-sugar strings -

RAGUENEAU (*admiringly*):   to heighten the taste!
                      It looks as though it could almost be played.
  (*To Apprentice 1*) My child, you have a future in this trade.

  (*The vivacious Lise enters carrying a stack of collapsed
  funnel-like white paper bags with writing all over them.*)

LISE: Husband!

RAGUENEAU (*proudly displaying
  the confection*): What do you think, Lise?

LISE (*considering*): I don't know.
                      (*Then quickly*) Give me a piece.
  (*She carelessly breaks a chunk off.
  Apprentice 1 gasps and collapses into the arms
  of the other apprentices, as Lise pops it into her mouth.*)
                              Not as good as that crumpet
                                  in the form of the trumpet.
  (*Apprentice 1 runs off, crying. Noticing not this, but the
  tablecloths scattered on the floor, Lise slams the bags
  down on a table.*)   Ragueneau,
                              it's time to open, and look at this mess!
  Have you been drinking again?

RAGUENEAU: No!
(He quickly, on the sly, hands off the bottle to
Apprentice 3 who similarly hands it off to
Apprentice 2 who likewise hands it off...to Lise.
She gives her husband a withering look.)

                                                    Well, not in excess.

(He hiccups and leans his arm on a table for support.
His hand slips off and he falls to the floor. The two
remaining apprentices lift him to his feet.)

LISE: You two!

(The apprentices drop their master and rush at once to
their mistress, one on each side of her - close on each side.)

BOTH APPRENTICES: Yes, Madame?!

LISE *(referring to Ragueneau)*: Oh, good!
        Something more on the floor. What is there left to drop?

RAGUENEAU: The subject?

LISE *(pushing them away)*: Go. Pick up the drunken sop.

BOTH APPRENTICES *(doing so)*: Yes, Madame.

LISE: But *first* pick-up this shop!

(They shrug to each other, drop their master again,
and set about picking-up the tablecloths and
generally tidying the premises.)

LISE *(to Ragueneau)*:   How is it that one can be so oblivious?
                Husband of mind, you have no head for business.

RAGUENEAU *(slowly picking himself up off the floor)*:
                    Then all the better, dear Lise, you do.
                    And look, how very clever of you,
to have made paper bags *(and in shocked recognition)*
                    ...out of my *Poems!?* My *Songs!?!*

LISE: You do say it's with the masses your work belongs.

RAGUENEAU: Packages for pastries!?!
                         Wife, is that how you regard my art?
            Oh, once again the wild Baccantes tear Orpheus apart!
      What a way to use Poetry!

LISE *(to Apprentice 3, sarcastically)*: Is there any better,
                                    do you suppose?

RAGUENEAU *(to 2)*: If she could do this to poesie,
                    Heaven knows what she would do with prose!
            (To his wife, sternly) Lise, one might well infer -

(The bell rings. Musketeer 1 enters.)

LISE: Sorry dear, customer!
            ...Bonjour, Monsieur. Can I help you...in any way?

MUSKETEER *(liking what he sees)*: Perhaps you may.
                    I am looking for something say -
                    sweet...and hot.

BOTH APPRENTICES: That we've got!

APPRENTICE 3: You'll just love the legendary Ragueneau Tart.

APPRENTICE 2 *(with a wink)*: Most everyone else has.

(Lise gives 2 a dirty look. The apprentice
holds up a tart – the baked sort.)

LISE *(snatching the tart away)*:   Apprentices, depart!

(They do so. Quickly.)

MUSKETEER *(suggestively)*: You know, I do enjoy a tasty tart.

LISE *(dropping the tart into one of her*
        pastry packages): My, not only handsome, but very smart.

(She hands him the bag, without letting go of it herself.)

RAGUENEAU *(not knowing what he wants more –*
his poem or his spouse): Then, Musketeer,
                why not eat it now? *(Aside to Lise)* Within my sight!
    (Grabbing the bag out of both of their hands) Here,
            dear *WIFE*, I'll take that bag; while you, sir, take a bite!
    (He shoves the tart in the Musketeer's mouth, brusquely
    seats the man at a table, then examines the bag.)
                Mon dieu, my poor "Sonnet to Carol Anne."
                    Let me try to read you, if I still can.
        (After smoothing the bag ever so gently, he reads
        sing-song from it.) "Oh, Carol Anne, your name I utter…"
                (Then flatly with dismay)
                    Then comes a big grease spot of butter!

(The bell over the door sounds again. Cyrano
enters hurriedly.)

CYRANO: What is the time?

RAGUENEAU: Seven or near.

*(Carrying two cups of coffee to the Musketeer's
table, Lise passes Cyrano and notices a wound.)*

LISE: Your hand?!

CYRANO *(covering it)*:   Bah. It is not severe.

LISE: What have you done now? How many lie dying?

CYRANO: Nothing. And None!

LISE: Un-huhn.
    (Then, sitting with the Musketeer): The man is lying.

CYRANO *(quietly to Ragueneau)*: Now,
    how does she always know?
    Does my nose begin to grow?!

                          Only joking; impossible, that.

RAGUENEAU *(confidentially)*: As was last night's
                          immortal combat.
    (Taking a quill pen from his hat or pocket)
            Indeed, your exploit inspires an epic poem!
    (Then, with a glance at the bag and at Lise)
            Though maybe it's best I do not work at home.

CYRANO: Wherever and when you begin your rhyme,
                first tell me again, Ragueneau - the time!

RAGUENEAU: Cyrano, ten seconds
    cannot have passed since you've come in.

CYRANO *(pacing nervously)*: Yes. Sorry.

RAGUENEAU: Good heavens,
            you're near crawling out of your skin!
    (As Lise waves unnoticed for her husband's attention)
            Are you all right? Sit!   Is there anything I can do?

CYRANO *(pointing)*: Attend to Lise.

RAGUENEAU: Huhn?

CYRANO: Best check your apprentices, too.

RAGUENEAU: My apprentices?

CYRANO: I believe I smell an overdone gateau in the oven.

LISE *(calling)*: Ragueneau, be a dear...

MUSKETEER: A loaf!

LISE *(to Musketeer)*: Yes, but you must try
                            his famed Gateau Parisiene!

    (She snaps her fingers at Ragueneau.)

MUSKETEER *(holding up his cup)*: Oh,
    and bring more of this delicious house blend.

CYRANO: Who is that with Lise?

RAGUENEAU: It appears, a new friend.

CYRANO: Hmmph!

RAGUENEAU: Well said!

(He flashes his feather pen, sword-like, at the Musketeer.)

CYRANO: Oh, might I borrow that quill?

RAGUENEAU: Why not? First unmanned…
              (handing it over) and now unpenned. Still -

CYRANO *(seating himself at the second table, trying to
concentrate)*: Shh! *(Ragueneau rolls his eyes and exits
to check the oven. Cyrano continues, to himself)*
     I'll have to *write* to her, put it in her hands, and go.
  Well, I guess that's all there is to it; I just do not know
     if I can speak one word
       to her. What a coward!
  How is it I can confront heinous cut-throats by the dozen,
        yet be too lily-livered to face my own gentle cousin?
          (Calling off to Ragueneau) What time now, Ragueneau?

RAGUENEAU *(returning with the charred and
       smoldering remains of a cake)*: Time to serve the gateau.

   *(Which he does, plopping it between his wife and the
   Musketeer, before heading to the final table with a
   very satisfied smile.)*

LISE *(a bit too sweetly,
         waving the smoke away)*: The loaf? We're waiting!

RAGUENEAU *(even more sweetly in return)* Yes, dear!
                    (Then, under his breath): Castrating -

   *(He lobs a slice off a baguette with one fell swoop
   of a large cutting knife.)*

CYRANO *(to himself)*:
  Since I find I cannot face her, surely I may still attest
of my true love by means of a letter.
                        Yes, that would serve me best –
  the missive I have composed already
            a hundred times or more within my heart.
  I need only commit it to the page,
                  and all my sentiments I can impart.
…But why is she so late?!

MUSKETEER *(to Lise)*: And to think, I almost didn't stop.

CYRANO *(to self,
  but overheard by Ragueneau)*: It must be nearly eight!

MUSKETEER *(to Lise)*: The street's in turmoil
                        around your shop.

CYRANO *(to self)*: Well, something's delayed her;
                        that's a *fait accompli.*

MUSKETEER *(to Lise)*: An incident nearby
                        at the Porte Saint-Denis.

CYRANO *(to self)*: Or perhaps –
                  perhaps, just as I am, she is afraid.

MUSKETEER *(to Lise)*: To think of the frightful carnage
                        on that promenade!

CYRANO *(to Ragueneau who is crossing with a
  tray of bread slices and coffee for Lise and her
  "customer")*: Ragueneau, the time?

RAGUENEAU: Little has passed,

Cyrano, since the last that you asked.
Will you please just relax, it's nowhere near **eight**!

MUSKETEER *(to Lisa, his first word spoken*
              simultaneously to Ragueneau's last): **Eight**
                    I counted! All of who met a gory fate.

LISE *(suspiciously to her husband)*: Ragueneau,
  were you mixed up in this?
                    Have your fool scribblings caused more trouble?

RAGUENEAU *(feigning indignity)*: The very thought!
  (He bangs the tray down. Then, aside to the Musketeer)
Was it only eight dead? Hmm, I must have been seeing double.

  (He crosses back to his work, upstage at his table.)

CYRANO *(to self)*:   But now to write.

  (He licks the quill point.)

MUSKETEER *(to Lise)*: But what a sight!

CYRANO *(writing)*:   I love you."

MUSKETEER *(continuing to Lise)*:   I hate to
      even tell you of it.
    This tale is hardly fit
      for -

CYRANO: "…your eyes…"

MUSKETEER: Scattered across the cobblestone –

CYRANO: "…your…"

MUSKETEER: blood, guts, even two –

CYRANO: "…lips…"

MUSKETEER: severed to the bone!
  I am told *one* man alone, by his sword's might,
      put a hundred rogues and ruffians to flight.
        Consider! A solitary being dispersing some mad revel?
  I tell you, Lise, this was not a man, but indeed the very devil!

CYRANO: "…a true angel…"

LISE: One hundred fell?

MUSKETEER: Yes!

LISE: No!

MUSKETEER: Dear Mademoiselle –

CYRANO: "…pray tell…"

MUSKETEER *(with a nod to*
  the smoldering cake): I would far sooner bake in hell
        than be caught in the same room
  with one whose wrath invokes such doom.
  (To self) One might well imagine
           the terrors his presence would bespeak.

CYRANO: "…Yet finding myself near,
          looking upon you, my knees grow weak.
  Your Friend – one who forever worships you."

MUSKETEER: Still, I do wonder who he is.

LISE: Me, too.

(They look at each other, and then at Cyrano.)

CYRANO: No need to sign it, for it's my plan
                   to hand it in person to Roxane.
*(He blows on the ink, folds the letter, and pockets it. He then
crosses with the quill to Ragueneau, who nibbles absently on
the paste lyre, unable to take his eyes off his wife and her
customer.")*   Thank you for the feather.

RAGUENEAU: Look at them, together.

CYRANO: Well, don't stand for it.
                              Chase him out, and make it snappy!

RAGUENEAU: Oh, but I mustn't, Cyrano; she looks so happy.

CYRANO: I like you, Ragueneau.

*(He slaps the man on his back. Ragueneau practically
chokes on a mouthful of lyre.)*

RAGUENEAU: You do? Even though
        at the art of song – to say naught of marriage –
                                    I am a pure disaster.

CYRANO: Oh, on the contrary, dear Ragueneau,
                                I find you the purist master,
    for art is only pure when done, not for Fortune,
        but from Love, as yours is.

RAGUENEAU: From Love? Well, yes…mainly.

CYRANO: Yet look at the artful treasure you hold in hand.

RAGUENEAU: Ha! At last the poet's lyre does sustain me!
(He takes another mouthful, then) Forgive my rudeness;
I've not offered you a bite.

CYRANO: Thank you, my "rich" friend, but I have no appetite
…except for my dear cousin's company.

RAGUENEAU: You're expecting Roxane?

CYRANO: Imminently.

RAGUENEAU: Oh, is that the reason you're so fidgety?

CYRANO *(with a fidgety nod)*: And I would
appreciate some privacy
when she arrives – if ever! Ragueneau, what time is it?

RAGUENEAU: Time perhaps for me
to scout out her impending visit.
(He exits through the upstage door.)

CYRANO: Lise! *(He signals her over with a wag of a finger.
She comes reluctantly.)* This Musketeer.
Tell me, is he trying to storm your barricades?

LISE: Stand down, Cadet.
I come fully well equipped to fend off any raids.

CYRANO: Your husband's a good soul.
They come no better in my gender.
So please do be certain you find no cause for sweet surrender.
(She turns away. He takes her arm.)
Madame, don't get too cozy.

LISE: Monsieur, don't be so – *Nosy*!

*(She breaks away and returns to her Musketeer who has briefly
locked eyes with Cyrano. He recoils at Cyrano's stare, and
Cyrano heads to the door. Lise confronts her "customer")*
                    How infuriating! You hear how that goes?!
                    You ought to punch that meddler right in the –

MUSKETEER: Don't even *say* it!

*(She angrily yanks him off-stage in one direction as
Apprentice 1 re-enters opposite, and briefly looks around.)*

APPRENTICE 1 *(to Cyrano)*: Sir, have you seen a lyre? *[liar]*.

CYRANO: Alas, only all too recently.

*(The apprentice finds his creation – half-eaten.
He begins to cry all over again.)*

RAGUENEAU *(re-entering)*: Monsieur de Bergerac –
  (With a flourish he admits Roxane and her Duenna).
     I'll now retire. *(To the ladies)*
                    Welcome to Ragueneau's Patisserie!

*(He starts off. Cyrano whistles. He returns and
tugs his apprentice off in the direction opposite
that of Lise's exit.)*

CYRANO: Come in! And "Good Day" to you both.

(He bows and stumbles, then clutches his knees.)

DUENNA *(to Roxane, giggling)*: His knees are wobbling,
                                        on my oath!

CYRANO: Roxane, with your Duenna may I have a word or two.

ROXANE *(playfully)*: A word or two?
                    Oh, I think as many as *four* – for you.

CYRANO *(to the Duenna,*
  counting each word with a finger): Do – you – like – cake?

DUENNA *(giggling)*:   For heaven's sake!

CYRANO *(grabbing a paper bag)*: Then here,
  be a glutton for some verse
                    in which Ragueneau has bared his soul.
  It's filled with éclairs *(- he puts some in)*,
    meringues *(- he puts some in)*, brioches
      (- he puts some in), bordures de pommes
      (- he puts some in), and *(- placing it on top -)* a jelly-roll!
  (He thrusts the bag upon her.)
        Now, do – you – like – Nature?

DUENNA: Of course, Monsieur.

CYRANO: Excellent! Then go eat these out the door!
  (He pushes her outside and slams the door
  behind her. He then re-opens it, and calls)
                    And don't come back until you're done!
    (He slams the door again. Then, to himself)
                    With each and *every* one.
    (Now, while escorting Roxane downstage,
    offering her a chair, and taking one himself) Roxane,
        henceforth this hour will be the most blessed of my day,
          for it is the one in which you have chosen to inveigh
  matters rather… "private," so it appears.
  I am happily – for a change – *all*…ears.

ROXANE: First, again for last night I am grateful.

That vile Vicomte – that creature –
                    whom your sword made ready sport…
Well, his "benefactor" –

CYRANO: De Guiche?

ROXANE: who thinks himself in love with me,
                    was to have this "puppet" purport
            to be my devoted - *surrogate* - groom.

CYRANO: To mask his own intentions, I presume.
     (She bows her head in embarrassed acknowledgment.)
            So much the better then for his demise;
     I fought, not for my nose, but your bright eyes.

ROXANE: And it is as such that I must thank-

CYRANO: Roxane. Not necessary. Not.
     But you…"desired" to meet with me this fine morning –
                    to tell me…what?

ROXANE: To tell you…*(She stands.)*
                    But before I can do so, I must see
        if you are still the same near-brother you used to be,
        when we would frolic and laugh and sing
                    in that garden such a long time back.

CYRANO *(rising also)*: I remember as if yesterday,
                    the summers you spent in Bergerac.

     *(He starts softly singing a childhood song of
     theirs. She joins in. Then)*

ROXANE: You made swords out of bullrushes, do you recall?

CYRANO: And you would weave dandelions into a shawl.

ROXANE: Oh, and the green leeks!

CYRANO: And the red mulberries –

ROXANE: that *you* squished –

CYRANO: to rouge your cheeks.

ROXANE: In those days, you did anything I wished.

CYRANO: Back then you were called Madeleine.

ROXANE: Was I pretty?

CYRANO: …Oh, not too plain.

ROXANE: Sometimes playing roughhouse with the boys,
                you'd hurt your hand one way or another.

CYRANO: Yes; then I'd come running straight to you.

ROXANE: And I would act the part of Mother -

CYRANO: An astoundingly brilliant pantomıme!

ROXANE: Thank you. *(She takes his hand.)* –
        and say *(in a deep maternal voice)*
                "What have you done this time?"
        (She looks at his hand, and is taken aback.)
                        Cyrano! What *have* you done?!

CYRANO: Just practiced some childhood fun;

I was playing roughhouse with the boys
                                            …at the Porte Saint-Denis.

ROXANE: At your age! Tsk-tsk-tsk. Here, let me see.

*(She sits him down, examines the wound,
and wets her handkerchief in a basin of water.)*

CYRANO: Still so motherly.

(She tends to his wound as they continue talking.)

ROXANE: So, tell me, sir, as I wash the blood away,
        with exactly how many boys did you…"play?"

CYRANO: Oh, only about a hundred so.

ROXANE: What?! You must tell me about it!

CYRANO: No.
      You must tell me what you came to tell – if you still dare.

ROXANE: Yes, Cyrano, I dare. Now that I know you still care.
     …I am in love with someone…

CYRANO: Ah.

ROXANE: …who does not know
       it, not at all.

CYRANO: Ah?

ROXANE: At least, I do not think so
        for, you see, I haven't told him yet.

CYRANO: Ah!

ROXANE: He loves me too, but is beset
    by shyness, so speaks to me not.
    Why, Cyrano, your hand is hot!

CYRANO: AH!

ROXANE: Oh dear, are you all right?
                   A bandage I should fashion.

(She begins wrapping his hand with her handkerchief.)

CYRANO: Ah.   …I am *more* than fine.
             Please go on about this…passion.

ROXANE *(considering)*: Yes, that is the word for it.
    (Confidentially) He is a Cadet.

CYRANO: Ah!

ROXANE: Of Gascony.

CYRANO: *Ah!*

ROXANE: And such a man. Noble
    (Quite pleased, Cyrano smiles, unnoticed) –
    Proud *(- another secret smile)* – full of unrivaled Bonhomie.
    (- yet another) - Oh, and *Beautiful* -

CYRANO *(turning pale, rising)*: Beautiful?

ROXANE: Cyrano, is something wrong?

CYRANO: No, nothing. …The hand.

ROXANE: Funny, I haven't even known him long,
                                    yet it does seem as if forever.

CYRANO: Not long?
(Roxane shakes her head.) But you have spoken?

ROXANE: Never.
    I've only looked upon him at the theater.
            But then, you might say we have spoken with our eyes.

CYRANO: Roxane, how can you possibly say that you know –

ROXANE: Cyrano, there are things one can not disguise,
        such as the intendment of the heart.
And people talk. That, too, plays a part.

CYRANO: What's his name? You say that he is a Cadet.

ROXANE: He is the Baron Christian de Neuvillette.

CYRANO: You are mistaken. I know no soldier of that name.

ROXANE: Well, of course not, cousin; he only recently came
    to Paris, and joins the ranks of the Cadets this very morning.

CYRANO: So quickly can we lose our hearts?

ROXANE: Sometimes even without warning.

CYRANO: My dear Roxane, a word of caution,
                                    for better or worse –

DUENNA *(entering)*: I have eaten all the cakes!

CYRANO *(indicating the empty paper bag)*: Good!

Now go digest the verse!
(He pushes her out the door, and returns to Roxane.)
Forgive me, but I know you as one who loves Poetry,
                        a Grand Spirit, and Wit.
How can you know if this stranger possesses any –
                        if even just a bit?
Tell me, my ingenuous cousin; what if his mind
            is no firmer than a *(picking one up)* – jelly roll?!

ROXANE: That cannot be, my cousin.
I have looked into his eyes, and in them I have seen his soul.

CYRANO: Yes. The soul may be written in the eye.
...But what if you are wrong?!

ROXANE: Then I shall die.

CYRANO *(after a pause)*: So,
            this is what you came to tell me? ...Why?

ROXANE: Upon whom else could I possibly rely?

CYRANO: Go on.

ROXANE: I am so afraid for Christian who is, in a way, alone.

CYRANO: How so?

ROXANE: Unlike the rest of the Cadets,
                    he is not of blood Gascon.

CYRANO: Ah, and you have heard –

ROXANE: It is well known –

CYRANO: that we are prone
                    to pick a quarrel with tender-foots not of our own?

ROXANE: And thus my fright.

CYRANO: Well…You are right.

ROXANE: So I thought – hoped – that if you, you who
                        yesterday was so invincible, you
                    whom all the Cadets so respect and fear –

CYRANO *(with a sigh)*:   I will protect your little baron dear.

ROXANE: And you will be his friend?

CYRANO *(with some distaste at the notion)*: Yes
                                        …to the bitter end.

ROXANE: And never let him fight a duel?

CYRANO: You have my word
                (- and under his breath) as a fool.

ROXANE: Cyrano de Bergerac, you are a darling!

DUENNA *(re-entering)*:   Mademoiselle!

ROXANE: I must go.
     Oh, but you never told me about last night!

CYRANO: Oh, well.

ROXANE: How you must have gone at it –

CYRANO: tooth and nail.

ROXANE: Have *him* write me – every last detail.
  Will you, Cyrano?

CYRANO: Of course.

ROXANE *(taking his hands)*:   Oh, I have always loved you!
  Well, dear Cousin, adieu. We are great friends, is it not true?

CYRANO: Yes.

ROXANE: Oh, he *must* write to me.
                    Cyrano, do make it be
                        so! *(She starts off, stops, and turns.)*
  One against a hundred. The very thought makes me wince.
    Such unheralded courage!

  (She exits with her Duenna.)

CYRANO: Oh, I have done better since.

  *(The door opens again. Le Bret hurries in,
  closing it quickly behind him.)*

LE BRET: Sorry, my friend.
                I've tried to fend
                        them off in every way.

  *(The door opens yet again. Cadet 1's
  head pops in. He calls down the street.)*

CADET 1: He's in here! *(To Cyrano)* Now, you stay!

  (He closes the door.)

LE BRET: News of your exploit has spread quickly.

Outside it's near a riot.
Oh, but what of Roxane?

CYRANO: At present, Le Bret, let us be quiet.

*(Cadets 1 and 2 storm into the shop one after the other.
3 and 4 get momentarily stuck in the door trying to go together. All are followed by some new compatriots - Cadets 5
and 6, who carry musical instruments.)*

CADET 1:   Cyrano!

CADET 2: Our hero!

CADET 3:   All of Paris sings your name!

CADET 4: You have brought us Gascons fame!

*(The repeated ringing of the bell over the door at each Ca-
det's entrance, along with the general commotion, has
brought Ragueneau, Lise, along with her Musketeer, back on
stage from opposite directions.)*

ALL CADETS *(singing loudly to instrumental accompaniment)*:
              We are the Cadets of Gascony –
                   The defenders of liberty.
            Beware lest we catch you in our sight,
               With eagle eyes and a wolf's –

LISA *(grabbing some baked-good out of one's hand)*: appetite!

ALL CADETS:
              We send to their final resting-place
                 All of those fool enough to face
            Who? - The Cadets of – *Where*? – Gascony!

(Each Cadet spears a roll with his foil and raises it in the air on the blade's point.)

RAGUENEAU *(into the spirit of things, spontaneously contributing a line)*: Hot blood is your true cup of tea!

(The Cadets cheer and flick their rolls into the audience or over their heads.)

LE BRET *(to Cadets 5 and 6)*: You should've seen it, boys, a glorious fight!

CADET 5: Sorry we missed it.

CADET 6: It was our bowling night.

CADET 1: The dust flew!

(He throws two handfuls of flour in the air.)

CADET 2:   The blood spilled!

(He pours two jars of jelly into a bowl.)

CADET 3: The bodies piled –

(He plops two globs of dough on the floor.)

CADET 4:   - Eight killed!
(He swings his sword, decapitating a baguette that is standing upright in a basket.) And, scurrying off like mice, some ninety-two more.

(All of the Cadets pretend to be swatting mice with their swords. Pastries fly!)

LISE *(clutching the remains of the beheaded baguette)*:
 Attention! *(Everything stops.)* Husband,
                                    show these Cadets the door
                 before they sack the whole store. Such a regiment!

RAGUENEAU: Indeed wife! Aren't they simply magnificent!

LISE *(to Musketeer)*: Shoot me. Shoot to kill.

MUSKETEER *(not even hearing the above)*:
                                    Cupcake, the devil
                 was de Bergerac!

*(She rolls her eyes, and crowns him on the head
with the baguette.)*

MAN OF LETTERS *(entering, with real urgency)*:
                                    Make way! Stand back!
                            I am with the Royal Almanac!
 Which one is Cyrano? *(Importantly)* My readers want to know!

(All point to Cyrano.)

CYRANO *(not pleased)*: Better they read Plato
                                    or Socrates. Now...Go.

(All point to the door.)

LE BRET *(pulling Cyrano by the sleeve)*:
 This is not a man to upset;
                 his paper can make or break your fame.

MAN OF LETTERS: Think banner headlines –
  (under his breath) across Page 2 –
                           big block letters spell your name –
S –Y – R – A –

CYRANO: N – O.

LE BRET: Listen to me. This is the Press!
Such publicity could at last spell long-overdue success.
 Holy Mother of God, man,
                    use your supposed intelligence –

CYRANO: To that I say "No Comment,"
                    what'er the consequence.
   (To the Man of Letters) You see, sir,
I frankly do not care for what your pages pass as news,

MAN OF LETTERS: Ah, but I also do the weather –
                    and the theatrical reviews!

LE BRET *(to Cyrano)*: How very odd to serve as
                    forecaster and critic collectively,

CYRANO: I can only guess the man
                    has a talent for inaccuracy,
for it's well known that weather-predictors
                    only half the time are right.
Critics, of course, fare half as well as that,
                    notwithstanding their hindsight.
What his sort doesn't know, you see,
                    it simply fabricates.

MAN OF LETTERS: Might I remind you,
      monsieur, that my sort decides men's fates.

CYRANO: I suppose the Church will have to adjust.
           Oh, very well; I do have news I trust
that you can use: My sword, kept sharp
                    with frequent parrying and thrust,

had been still, sir, this entire morning.
                              its blade begins to rust!

*(He reaches for it. The Man of Letters flees,
Ragueneau opening the door for him. There, the
baker notices something on the street and shuts
the door quickly.)*

RAGUENEAU: Uh-oh! The Comte de Guiche comes on
                                            his chair!

DE GUICHE *(or rather his VOICE, off-stage, but clearly
in motion, crossing from one side to the other, upstage of
the Pattiserie wall)*: Put me down! Put me down, I say!
                                            ...Right there!

*(A bang and a groan are heard. A pause. De Guiche enters,
rubbing his rump; angry and sore.)*

LISE: How may we serve you, sir? Something to drink?
                              Something to eat?

RAGUENEAU: Perhaps Monsieur would just prefer
                              a pillow for his seat?

(De Guiche, suddenly conscious of his rubbing, stops.)

DE GUICHE: No thank you.
I am here having been sent to find de Bergerac, not to hob-nob.

CYRANO *(stepping forward)*: And might this visit perhaps
                  concern the fate of a certain unfortunate mob?

DE GUICHE *(coldly)*: Indeed so.
  Sir, the Marshall has charged me to convey his compliments -

*(a long collective "Ooooh!" from the very impressed
Cadets, which de Guiche quickly stifles with a stare)*
        on your singular act of subduing the very malcontents
you have just mentioned.

RAGUENEAU: Ha-ha! Just like a cook,
                                                        he made them all mincemeat!

*(Laughter. Cyrano bows perfunctorily, staring the
Cadets down himself.)*

CYRANO: It appears it was not possible
                                            to keep this incident...discreet.

LE BRET *(aside to Cyrano)*: What is wrong? You
should be delighted. The Marshall speaks with great authority.

CYRANO: Just now, Le Bret, were I to be knighted,
                                            it would matter not at all to me.

DE GUICHE: Furthermore, 'though I don't know why,
                                            your earlier "poetic" duel
seems to have amused my uncle, the Cardinal Richelieu, who'll
generously sponsor any verse plays
                        your fertile mind may have devised.

LE BRET: Cyrano, at last,
you will have that piece of yours produced!

CYRANO: Or compromised!

DE GUICHE: The Cardinal, as you well know,
                                            is himself a dramatist.
He will rewrite a line or two, but not alter the gist
of it.

LE BRET *(to Cyrano, excitedly)*: They say Richelieu pays
                    quite handsomely when he sanctions a drama.

CYRANO: My pride would pay a fair steeper price
                    were I to let him change one comma.

LE BRET: Indeed, this pride of yours
                                        may one day cost you dearly.

*(Cadet 7 enters with a string of hats impaled on
his sword. All have rather bedraggled plumes.)*

CADET 7: Ah, Captain Le Bret!
                    Look what I've just found. Why, clearly,
Cyrano, these are the spoils of your last night's storied hunt –
the molted feathers of those "fowl" fellows you did confront.

(Laughter. Cheers. Some "clucks.")

LE BRET: Those poor one hundred capons!
                    To be pitilessly pounced upon by one Gascon fox.

RAGUENEAU: *Always* count your chickens,
    boys, before you hatch…a plot!

LE BRET *(to de Guiche)*: You'd have laughed, sir,
                                        to hear their squawks.

DE GUICHE: I think that rather unlikely.

CYRANO: Ah. You see,
    gentlemen, the one who loosed those hens –

DE GUICHE: was me.
    (The laughter, etc. stops.) Alas,

too hastily, I engaged that regrettably worthless band
since, as a rule, I typically refrain from soiling my own hand
with this sort of thing.

CYRANO: Oh? That "sort" being
what exactly?

DE GUICHE *(closing in on Ragueneau)*: The teaching
of a lesson to a perfidious fool poet!

LISE *(closing in on her husband opposite)*: Un-huhn.
So, this *was* all your fault, you meddlesome crumb!
How ever did I know it?!

RAGUENEAU *(cowering)*: Next song I write,
you'll be the first to whom I show it.

LISE: Ragueneau, if you dare write another, I shall throw it
in the oven – and you, husband, right after!

RAGUENEAU: I only mean to give a little laughter.

CYRANO *(to the baker,*
while taking Cadet 7's sword): And so you have,
dear artist Ragueneau, and so you will!
Indeed, please favor us now with a small poetic "frill."
(In a gesture of saluting de Guiche with the sword,
he slides all of the hats onto the floor at the
Comte's feet. To de Guiche) Sir, a trophy.
Perhaps you'd care to return it to your coterie –
(Handing Ragueneau the sword, he gestures for
the "frill.")

RAGUENEAU: all those Port Saint-Denis "chickens"
Cyrano turned *chicken fricassee*!

*(Laughter and applause, though not from either
Lise or de Guiche, the latter of whom stops the
ruckus with a sharp turn of his head.)*

DE GUICHE *(maintaining his self-control, smiling)*: As for
        you, monsieur, have you read Cervantes' *Don Quixote*?

CYRANO: I have *lived* it, sir, and so,
                    of course, am a great devotee.

DE GUICHE: Then might I suggest
             you read again Chapter Thirteen.

CYRANO: About the windmills.
               And doing so, what might I glean;
            that my enemies change with every wind?

DE GUICHE: What you may glean, sir – and shall be chagrined
  to hear – is this: When you battle windmills,
        they may swing their mighty spars,
  and cast you down into the mud.

CYRANO: Or, then again, up – among the stars!

DE GUICHE *(shouting to no one in particular)*: Call me
  a sedan chair!

(The Cadets all look at each other, shrug, and)

ALL CADETS *(to de Guiche, bowing)*: Sir,
                 you are a "Sedan Chair!"

(De Guiche storms out the door.)

DE GUICHE *(or rather his off-stage VOICE)*:
  Porters, here! *(After a beat)* Now go! No!
                        Wait 'til I – Stop, or I swear –
(After a pause, the door opens) Tonnerre!
  Why, no sooner had I tossed my purse in there,
than those idiots were off! ...Has anyone cab fare?

(All look to the floor, sheepishly. De Guiche
slams the door again, and is gone. While Lise and
the Musketeer occupy themselves otherwise,
Ragueneau and the Cadets run to the door to
enjoy the off-stage spectacle.)

CADET 7: Look at de Guiche go! He's already past our quarters.

CADET 3: All the same,
                  five sous says he'll never catch those porters.

CADET 1:   No bet here. Those boys know all too well
           that if he catches them...

CADET 2:   ...they'll catch hell.

CADETS 5 & 6: Go, sedan chair, go!

RAGUENEAU: Of which "chair" is it
                  do you suppose they speak?

CADET 4: Don't know, *(and to Cadet 3)*
  but my money's on the Comte, Cadet. He runs a blue streak!

(Cadets 3 and 4 shake on the wager. Le Bret and
Cyrano have remained downstage, apart from the others.)

LE BRET: You never cease to amaze me.

Are you completely crazy?
Hmpf, I am beginning to see your future quite clearly – None!

CYRANO: Oh, stop growling, Le Bret,
                              or I too shall call a chair and run.

LE BRET: But, Cyrano, why do you insist on ruining
                              every chance that comes your way?

CYRANO: What would you have me say?
                    That I should cling to an all-powerful patron's pay
        as though it were a tree, and I some crawling vine?
        No thank you! Or scratch the back of any old swine
        that will root up the truffles on which I might dine?
        No thank you. Fill pages to paper Mammon's shrine,
                              or dedicate, as the others do,
        poems to pawnbrokers? Well, no thank you.
            Callous my hands towing someone else's line,
        or, by bowing and kowtowing, curve my spine?
            Rip my belly groveling in the dust?
        Again, no thank you. I decline. I must.
        Should I scheme? Or so tremble
                  to affront, that I confine my art?
        Seek introductions and favors,
                    and so thusly consign my heart?
            Ask me, good sir, if I can conceive of any fate worse
        than loving more to make a visit than to make a verse?
            And I say:
            No Thank You! *No Thank You!* …I had rather not.

LE BRET: I see. Well, if that is so,
                              Monsieur de Bergerac; then tell me what?

CYRANO: To dream, to laugh, to sing,
                    to let my heart take wing,

Free! - with an eye open to see all things as they are!
 To fight – to write – to follow the moon or any star
      I choose
  - win or lose -
        to say onto myself: "Cyrano,
  be contented with whate'er you grow –
      be it flower, fruit, or – yes, even – weed,
        so long as it is planted from *your* seed."
        In short, the only garden I will harrow is my own.
And if it stands not high, well then at least it stands Alone!

LE BRET: Alone, yes! But why stand against the world?
 (The Cadets begin returning to the tables, Ragueneau
      serving them.) Why fly that flag of bitter pride unfurled?
 What of your love for enemies, one might ask.
 I presume this scornful face you wear a mask -

CYRANO *(interrupting)*: A mask? Ha!
               There's none yet made to fit.

LE BRET: - concealing feelings you won't admit.

CYRANO: Utterly ridiculous!

LE BRET: But true.
 (Taking Cyrano's arm; gently) Tell me,
      my friend, does she not love you?

 (The bell over the door rings. Christian enters as
 Cyrano, hushing Le Bret, hauls him into a back room.)

CHRISTIAN: Ah, as reported, you are safe and sound,
                     friend Ragueneau.
 But did you know around your corner there is quite the show?
 A very winded Comte de Guiche

is putting two porters on a leash.
(An annoyed Cadet 3 slaps five sous into the
open palm of Cadet 4.) Well, it seems that
               to find the Cadets this *is* the place to come!

CADET 7: Most observant, stranger.
               Yes, there are some days we like to slum.

(Laughs.)

LISE *(flirting)*:   Monsieur, may I take your order?

CHRISTIAN *(in all innocence)*: Ragueneau,
                         is this your daughter?!

LISE *(beaming)*: Who's Ragueneau?

MUSKETEER: Take your business elsewhere, sir.
               Madame Lise already has a customer.

(He yanks Lise away.)

RAGUENEAU: Cadets of Gascony, one and all!
               A new "slave" to join you in your thrall.
               I know you will make him feel at home and most well met.

CHRISTIAN *(flourishing his sword)*: At your service;
                         Baron Christian de Neuvillette.

CADET 7: Christian "De Neuvillette"?
                         That is not a *Gascon* name.

CHRISTIAN: No, I come from North of Cascony,
                         but all the same –

CADET 1: When you say "North" of Gascony,
                                you are not suggesting – "Above"?

CADET 2: Best be careful what you say, outsider,
                                or you might taste my glove.

CADET 3: Have you even a clue what we Gascons
                                are capable of?

CADET 4: Should we tell of Cyrano's hundred
        (- He takes Christian's hat and plays with its plume -)
                                or might that scare the dove?

CHRISTIAN *(grabbing his hat back)*: Dove?

CADET 7: Hark, he sings!
                But you'd better watch your *Northern* tune,
        little bird, or we will plant you six feet *South* most soon.

RAGUENEAU: Boys!
    Don't you think that since Cyrano has now been given mention,
        perhaps you best bring "You-Know-What"
                                to this newcomer's attention.

CADET 1 *(reluctantly)*: Oh, all right.
                        If you value your life, de Neuvillette,
        there is one small -

ALL OTHER CADETS: Large!

CADET 1:   - thing that you must not forget.

CADET 2: There is a subject

MUSKETEER: - well, more an "object" –

(They all look at him. He retreats.)

CADET 2:   of which we never speak.

CADET 3: In effect, a certain "aspect" of our Cyrano -
                                            quite...unique.

(An awkward silence.)

CHRISTIAN: Well, what is it? Is it something you'll disclose?

CADET 4 *(making certain the coast is clear)*: Look,
Northerner – *(They all tap their noses three times.)* Understand?

CHRISTIAN: Oh! You mean his –

ALL CADETS: Don't say it!!!

RAGUENEAU *(wiping his brow)*: Oh, mon dieu.

CADET 1:   To even breathe the word is banned.

CHRISTIAN: One word?

CADET 2:   One syllable! -

CADET 3:   One sound! -

CADET 4:   A single sneeze too loud,
   and the handkerchief you draw becomes your burial shroud.

*(Cyrano and Le Bret return, not yet noticing Christian.
The Cadets immediately try to look busy and nonchalant.)*

CHRISTIAN *(to Ragueneau)*: Tell me, friend,
what's the best thing to do when these Southerners give you hell?

RAGUENEAU: Simple, Christian. Prove to them
                    that Northerners can "dish" it out as well.

(This spoken as he hands Christian a dish of pastries.)

CADET 5: Cyrano, for those of us who missed it,
                        do tell of last night's glory!

CADET 6: Yes, please, in your very words,
                        the whole of the illustrious story!

(Cyrano looks toward Le Bret.)

LE BRET *(encouraging)*: Do so, old friend;
                    it may distract you from your melancholy.

CADET 7: Come, Cyrano –
                the true account of the Comte de Guiche's folly!
...And we'll not have you skimp on any details.

CYRANO: My story? Very well.
                (With his old bravado) Cyrano regales!
    *(Everyone eagerly clusters around him, except Christian
        who sits apart.)*
    I set forth, a full moon hanging overhead
                            like a golden watch within its case,
    when suddenly an angel rubbed a cloud across its glass,
                            as though to wash its face.
    So darkness fell, the night now black as ebony,
    and, indeed, in such obscurity, I could not see –

CHRISTIAN: further than your *nose*.

(Dead silence. Everyone slowly gets up, looking a Cyrano in abject terror. On his part, Cyrano is utterly dumbfounded.)

CYRANO: Who is that man? *(All are speechless. With his eyes fully fixed on Christian, Cyrano grabs the nearest Cadet.)*
                                        Are you deaf...or mute?
Who – is – he?
   Answer me *(- turning his glare on his captive -)* NOW!

CADET *(trembling uncontrollably)*:   A...a...a...a new recruit
                          as of this m...m...m...m...morning.

MUSKETEER: They did try to give him fair warn-

(Without so much as a glance in his direction, Cyrano swings his sword at the intruding Musketeer who escapes a beheading only by a timely duck.)

CYRANO *(continuing)*: His name?

CADET: I...I...I...I...I forget.

RAGUENEAU: The Baron Christian de Neuvil-
         (Cyrano turns pale, and drops the Cadet.) ...lette?

CYRANO *(gesturing "Enough" with the hand that just released his victim)*: Ah! *(He flushes, then regains control of himself.)*
   I...I...see. Very well then. ...As I was saying,
   (- with a sudden burst of rage) Black grew the skies!
      ...And in such obscurity,
                  I could not see...my *hand* before my eyes.
   But I marched on thinking how pleased I was
                                    that for a friend's sake
      I might be offending some noble who could easily break –

CHRISTIAN: your *nose*?

*(All rise, except Christian who remains most casual,
pleased to be "dishing" it out to a Gascon.)*

CYRANO *(half-strangled)*: my *reputation*.
                              Yes, in this way
   I'd be provoking one who could make me pay -

CHRISTIAN: *through the nose.*

CYRANO *(wiping the sweat from his brow)*: *pay –*
                        the piper, and continued on
                  never stopping once to consider anon
   was it wise to stick my –

CHRISTIAN: *nose*?

CYRANO: *finger* in the pie;
      the quarrel not being one of my own.
   It was then the villains cast the first stone.
      A sword flashed in the night's pitiless shade.
   I caught it fair –

CHRISTIAN: *on the nose!*

CYRANO *(shaking)*:   *on my blade!*
   Before I knew it, why, there I stood against the hordes –

CHRISTIAN: *rubbing noses!*

CYRANO: *crossing swords*,
      a score of them upon me!
      The scum of this hard city.
   Instantly, I picked my –

CHRISTIAN: *Nose!*

CYRANO: my *first* of a hundred foes,
                         and handed him –

CHRISTIAN: a *nose*gay.

CYRANO *(bursting)*: *Ventre-Saint Gris*!

*(Everyone bolts out of the room in one
direction or another.)*

MUSKETEER: Out of my way!

(Other lines are lost in the commotion, until)

LE BRET *(the last out)*:   The poor man is dead.

CHRISTIAN *(after surveying an empty room)*: Was it
                              something I said?

*(Cyrano strides towards him. Christian
rises and puts his hand to his sword.)*

CYRANO: De Neuvillette...
     (After a brief face-off) Come into my arms!

CHRISTIAN: Sir?

CYRANO: You have courage. It has its charms.

CHRISTIAN: This response...?

CYRANO: You were expecting some other?

CHRISTIAN: Quite so.

CYRANO: Do you not know? - I am her brother.

CHRISTIAN: Whose?

CYRANO: Hers. ...Roxane's!

CHRISTIAN: Do tell!
    Can it be?   Her brother!

*(Christian hurls himself upon Cyrano.
They embrace.)*

CYRANO: Well,
            in fact, her cousin, but near as close.

CHRISTIAN: But should this then lead me –

CYRANO: by the *nose*?

CHRISTIAN: - to conclude that she has told you...?

CYRANO: All!

CHRISTIAN: Then did she say...?

CYRANO: "Say"?

CHRISTIAN: That is... - Does she love me?!

CYRANO: Well, Christian...so she may.

CHRISTIAN: I am so happy I could cry!

(He vigorously embraces Cyrano again.)

CYRANO *(indicating his nose)*: Careful,
                              you could poke out an eye.
   (Holding Christian at arm's length) Yes,
              you do have a handsome face.

CHRISTIAN: Sir, my remarks were out of place.
   I beg you to forgive me, and please accept my true respects.

CYRANO: As Roxane would have me do,
                         but be informed what she expects
      of you.

CHRISTIAN: And what is that, pray tell?

CYRANO: Only a letter.

CHRISTIAN: Not from me?!
            Then I may as well have never met her.
               All is lost! If I write her, I am ruined.

CYRANO: A simple letter such a mortal wound?
      Why?

CHRISTIAN: Because I am a slow-witted fool!
                                   My romance done.

CYRANO: No, dear boy,
                      for a true fool never sees himself as one.
         And your remarks to me were not those of a fool.
      They were...*(a begrudging admission)*
                         vaguely clever sorts of ridicule.

CHRISTIAN: Oh, I can pick a fight.

With men, I have a soldier's ready tongue.
But when I am "up against" a woman,
                    my words come all unstrung.
Would that I had the way to say
what's here *(indicating his heart)* with any kind of grace.

CYRANO: Whereas I do have the words to speak,
                    but lack the comely face.
*(He looks intently at Christian, a plan
beginning to percolate.)* If only my soul had a fitting interpreter.

CHRISTIAN: I know how you feel!
                    If only somehow I could bestir
          your dazzling eloquence and wit.

CYRANO: Well, Christian, why not borrow it?
  And, in return, you can lend me
          your winning physicality.
    My dear boy, before us lies an extraordinary chance.
    Think of it, the *two* of us become *one* hero of romance!

CHRISTIAN: What?

CYRANO: Tell me, could you learn to say
          words I might give you day by day?

CHRISTIAN: You mean…?

CYRANO: I mean with you and I in collusion,
          Roxane needs not endure any disillusion.

CHRISTIAN: But Cyra —

CYRANO: What say you, Christian?
          What of your great yearning?

CHRISTIAN: Cyrano, your eyes?
  It seems almost as though they're burning.
    Does this wooing of Roxane matter so to you?

CYRANO *(besides himself)*: Deeply!
  (Catching himself, he changes his tone)
        Well, that is, from a certain point of view.
                It is, you see, the ultimate exercise of my art.
    A playwright's words are dead until an actor speaks the part.
    So come, what say you of our proposed collaboration –
        your beautiful facade and my soul's articulation?

CHRISTIAN: Yes, but as for this letter I'm supposed to send -

CYRANO *(taking from his pocket the one that he has
      written)*: Here. All done but for your signature at the end.
  (Handing it over) I think you'll find it most affecting.

CHRISTIAN: But how's –

CYRANO: Oh, we poets find amusement writing vows
        to enchanting creatures of our fanciful ideal.
  Far better that you give it to someone who is real.

CHRISTIAN: But without a word or two of alteration,
                              will it fit Roxane?

CYRANO: Trust me, good Christian de Neuvillette,
                    like her own glove upon her hand.

CHRISTIAN *(once again throwing himself
  into the arms of Cyrano)*: My friend!

  *(They stand in an embrace. The door opens a little.
  Ragueneau steals in.)*

RAGUENEAU *(to the others still outside)*: Nothing.

Silent like a tomb.

I hardly dare look about the room.

(He spots the two, and can't believe his eyes.
Loudly) Merde!?

(With the possible exception of Cadets 5, 6, [if they are dou-
bling as the pages in the next scene] and 7 [if he is doubling
as an apprentice] everyone begins cautiously crowding into
the room from various directions.)

CADET 1:   What! I don't believe it!

CADET 2: Who would ever conceive it?

CADET 3: So it took a "Christian"

to convert our devil to a Holy Brother,

CADET 4: who, struck on one nostril, has now,

apparently, learned to turn the other.

MUSKETEER: Well, well, well. Seems we need

no more concern ourselves with suffering losses

to life and limb when ridiculing him

about that prolonged proboscis.

(He has a plan. Calling) Lise! Attend. You may enjoy this.

(He gives her a wink, then continues in a manner that
can't help but grab everyone's attention.) Ca peu!

What is that horrid stink?

(With exaggerated sniffing, he ultimately plants
himself directly in front of Cyrano, and stares most
impolitely at his nose.) Oh, Cyrano!

Am I glad you're here. What can it be, do you think?

If anyone can tell, it's you – with that preposterous snout!

Why, I'd guess a smell like that is strong enough to –

CYRANO (knocking the Musketeer
                    head over heels): knock you out?

(Pandemonium! Joy! The old Cyrano is back. Off-stage music – playing and singing ostensibly by the Cadets and apprentices - accompanies the scene change. The Cadets clear
the stage in a choreographed dance that ends with the Baker
Apprentices carrying away the unconscious Musketeer – perhaps carting him off on the last of the rolling tables.
Ragueneau, still brandishing the sword that skewered the
hats, displays a new courage, handing Lise a broom and indicating the mess that needs sweeping. She chases him off-
stage with it.)

Scene iii: Roxane's Kiss

(The music begins to gradually deteriorate as the shift completes to the new setting – the exterior of the home of Roxane. Her Duenna is seated on a bench beside the front door
that, itself, is perhaps recessed in a small arched alcove. She
is arranging flowers plucked from the scattered plantings
around the house. Above the door is a French window that
opens onto a balcony. The window is framed by outrageously
long drapes that hang right down to the ground. The leafy
top of a Jasmine tree hangs in the sky near the house, its
green canopy covered in French script. A huge highly articu-
lated moon suggests the time – early evening. Cyrano enters
the scene followed by two pages with their theorbos [or other
period stringed instruments]. This entrance reveals that it is
they who have been singing and playing – badly – through
the latter part of the scene change.Cyrano stops in his tracks
and shakes his head.)

CYRANO *(turning on the pages)*: No, no, no!
  (The pages stop playing and singing.)

DUENNA: Oh, Monsieur! I thought we were to have a serenade.

CYRANO: Indeed, Madame, that was my plan and purpose.
                                        But I am afraid
    that these poor pages can not tell a C-Sharp from a B-Flat.

DUENNA: From what book are such pages torn?

CYRANO: None I'd write. *(Much frustrated,
  he grabs an instrument away from one of the pages and
        demonstrates its proper handling.)* Hold it like...That!

ROXANE *(stepping out onto the balcony,
  her vision somewhat obscured by the tree)*: Who's there below?

CYRANO *(playing the instrument
                        and singing waggishly)*: I, Cyrano,
    to praise your roses, lilies, and cowslips,
    and, most exquisite of all...your "two lips."

ROXANE: Ha-ha. I'll be down soon.

CYRANO *(as she returns inside)*: I'll wait.

DUENNA: Better yet, why not "orchestrate"
    a quick exit.

CYRANO *(to the pages, demonstrating; but not
  before giving the Duenna a nasty smile)*: You see,
                            this is the proper fingering.
  (They are not particularly interested.) Now,

pay close attention, I say, and no malingering
for I promise if you don't "**see** sharp" you *will* "**be** flat!"

DUENNA: And to think to string those things,
                                they wasted a good cat.

(The pages try and fail to duplicate Cyrano's fingering.)

CYRANO: La! What do you two have for brains –
                                sour cream and cottage cheese!?

DUENNA: So, Cyrano,
                        where did you turn-up these dazzling prodigies?

CYRANO: I won them in a wager over a point of grammar.

DUENNA: Or lost, considering the cacophonous clamor
        they perform.

CYRANO: True. Theirs is a sad mockery of song.
        And yet still, these two pages are mine this whole day long.
        (Confidentially) That I shall not lose them sooner
                                counts high among my fears.
    I'm only grateful it's my nose that's large, and not my ears.
    Wait, I've an idea of musical "note." Pages!

BOTH PAGES: Yes, sir?

CYRANO: I want you to pay
        a visit to the actor, Montfleury.
            Tell him I sent you; then play away!

BOTH PAGES: Play what, sir?

CYRANO: Oh anything. Just play it often…

(The pages bow and exit, singing and playing.
                    Then, to the Duenna)   ...and off-key.

DUENNA: You'll kill the ham.

CYRANO: Shall I call them back?

DUENNA: No!   Better him than me.

ROXANE *(entering through her front door)*: Good evening,
   Cyrano. *(Noticing)* Oh, your pages! Gone? *(Both Cyrano
   and her Duenna nod. Disappointedly)*
                              And I had so hoped for a pavane.

CYRANO: And why is that?
   Are you perhaps of a temperament to dance tonight, Roxane?

ROXANE: Oh, yes! *(She takes Cyrano's hand, compelling
   him to dance with her through the following, humming
   joyfully between her lines.)* So, cousin,
                    what brings you here if not to dance?

CYRANO: Oh, just the usual, I suppose – to have a chance
          to ask after our friend so handsome and so skilled.

ROXANE: Ah, a precious lily one could no further gild.
   Christian is beautiful and brilliant and -

CYRANO *(with some pride)*: "Brilliant," you say?

ROXANE: As is this moon!
          Or, better still, that brighter orb of day.
   (The dancing stops.) Even more so, Cyrano, than you!

CYRANO *(clutching his chest, staggering)*: Ah,

Mademoiselle, I am slain. Adieu!
(To the Duenna, as he plants one of her flowers on his chest)
Madame, kindly plant my poor corpse in your flower bed.

*(The Duenna grabs the flower back and carries her
bouquet into the house. Roxane, paying his antics no
mind, continues.)*

ROXANE: No man has ever before so magnificently said
such dear near-nothings that import, oh, so much.
Strangely, he will sometimes falter, lose his touch,
but afterwards speak such art, it seems if by Grace divined!

CYRANO: Really?

ROXANE: I am surprised to find you of such narrow-mind,
to presume a man with a handsome face must be a fool.

CYRANO: And does he talk of love so eloquently, as a rule?

ROXANE: Cyrano, he does not talk, but rather rhapsodizes!

CYRANO: Ah, but can he write?

ROXANE: Oh, he only immortalizes
love with pen and ink!
*(The Duenna appears on the balcony, placing the flower
arrangement, but busy listening.)* Tell me what you think:
"Take my heart and I shall have it all the more.
What else in losing can one so possess?"

DUENNA *(wistfully)*: Ah, words like those
one waits a lifetime for.

CYRANO *(considering)*: Well, yes;
     perhaps in that line, some *small* success.

ROXANE *(dismissing him)*: I see. And what then of this:
     "Yet the ache of emptiness bids me seek
 your heart's abounding fill -"

CYRANO *(interrupting)*: Ah ha!
     Here, if you will, a humble critique:
 First he has too much, then too little heart.
     Just how much does he want!?

DUENNA: Why, there's your typical man for you!

ROXANE *(infuriated)*:   Yes, and a fine confidante!

DUENNA: He's jealous, that's what he is.

ROXANE: Obviously.

DUENNA: C'est la vie!

CYRANO: Jealous? Jealous of what?

ROXANE: But what else - his poetry!
   Just listen to this, such rare tenderness, such art –

CYRANO: Roxane, do you know all of these letters by heart?

ROXANE: Every last one of them.

CYRANO *(twisting his moustache)*: Why,
     that is rather flattering, indeed.

ROXANE: He is a master.

CYRANO: Master?

ROXANE & DUENNA: Yes!

CYRANO *(bowing)*: A master then. I do concede.

DUENNA *(noticing from her*
  high vantage point): Mademoiselle, the Comte de Guiche
                                is coming straight this way!

ROXANE *(to Cyrano)*: Quick! Inside the house.
                (To the Duenna) He has not seen us yet, I pray?
   (The Duenna shakes her head and goes inside.) Dear
cousin, were he to find you here, he might well grow suspicious.
  I fear what he might do to Christian; the man can be, well –

DUENNA *(appearing at the front door)*:   Vicious!

CYRANO *(indignantly)*:   Fine then, I'll go! But let me tell –

   (He is yanked into the house by the Duenna,
   who closes the door behind them. Roxane
   busies herself with some of the remaining flowers.)

DE GUICHE *(entering)*:   Roxane. I came to say farewell.

ROXANE: You're leaving Paris?

DE GUICHE: To besiege Arras,
   where France and Spain carry on their fight.
            My orders are to depart tonight.

ROXANE: For Arras.

DE GUICHE *(after a brief pause)*: But I see, to you,
    that is of no concern. My departure leaves you...cold.

ROXANE *(politely)*: Oh! Not that.

DE GUICHE: As for me, Roxane,
    every moment of my day, I will burn to hold
you in my arms.

ROXANE: Monsieur, I beg you, do not force my hand –

DE GUICHE: Did you know, my precious,
    that I have been given a command?

ROXANE: Bravo, sir. I hope of soldiers with backbones.

DE GUICHE: Oh, yes.
    Though many may end beneath headstones.

ROXANE: Who is this valiant force?

DE GUICHE: Why, the Gascons, of course,
    among whom your insufferable cousin serves.
And, who knows? He may soon just get what he deserves.

ROXANE: The Cadets go to war?

DE GUICHE: To hell.
With me their Colonel, Mademoiselle.

ROXANE *(sinking breathless onto the bench,
aside)*: Christian!

DE GUICHE: What was that?

ROXANE: This war...Oh, how it makes me despair
   to see it steal away one for whom I so deeply care.

DE GUICHE *(taken aback)*: The first you have spoken
                 thus to me, from the heart –
   but now on this, the very day I must depart.

ROXANE *(recovering)*: Tell me. Am I to understand
         that you intend to exact your revenge on Cyrano?

DE GUICHE: Why? Would you care?

ROXANE: No. Not for him.

DE GUICHE: Ah!

ROXANE: Because, if so, Comte,
        then there is something you should know.
  Little in this world would please my cousin more
    than to be sent into the fiery grip of war.
  In seeking vengence, that's the last thing I would do.

DE GUICHE: Oh? And what instead?

ROXANE: Simple, Colonel - Make him stew!
  Order him and his fellow Cadets to stay behind
  as all others go off to glory, and you shall find
 that while the rest of the Gascons sit and chew their nails,
   Cyrano eats out his heart – and so your plan prevails.

DE GUICHE: So you do love me then? Taking my side above
       his. I should like to see in that a sign of love.

ROXANE: Of love? Yes. At any and all cost.

DE GUICHE *(removing a dispatch from*
  a stack of them): Then, one set of marching orders – lost!
            (And as he pockets it separately)
  The Cadets of Gascony do not set-off tonight.
  So much for cousin Cyrano itching for a fight!
                      …Well now, even you play the game.

ROXANE: When I must.

DE GUICHE *(close to her, speaking hurriedly)*: Oh, I am aflame,
  my darling Roxane, to find at long last,
                      love trembling within you!
  Though I should leave with my troops,
              I know now instead what I must do.
  Near by, you know, is that old monastery run by the Capuchin
  Monks. As faithful servants of my uncle
                      they will hide me there within.
  And later – when everyone supposes I am gone –
  I will mask myself so that I might call upon
              you secretly for a long-awaited tryst.

ROXANE: Yes, but think if you were somehow to be missed,
  and found-out. What then of your honor,
                      your name, and reputation?

DE GUICHE: A pity!
          But what are they compared to my infatuation!

ROXANE: I must make it my duty
              to make you do yours. A hero
  is who I will have – Antoine!

DE GUICHE: My name!

ROXANE: On my lips…*(pushing him away)* as you go!

DE GUICHE: Then adieu, my dearest.
                    We shall meet again; you need not fret.
But think often of your love.

ROXANE: I will. I do.
        (He bows, kisses her hand, and exits.) ...de Neuvillette.

DUENNA *(entering from inside,*
    imitating Roxane): "A hero I will have – Antoine!"

ROXANE: Quiet!

DUENNA: Oh, relax; he is gone.

ROXANE: Did Cyrano hear?

DUENNA: He went straight to sleep; declaring de Guiche a bore.
    And let me tell you; I could barely hear.
                        Hmpf, the way that man can snore!

ROXANE: Thank heaven!
        He would never forgive me if he knew I stole his war.
    (Calling) Cousin! *(To Duenna)* Not a word!
    (Cyrano appears.) De Guiche is gone.

CYRANO: And Christian will soon arrive.
    I best be off. *(He starts to go, but stops.)*
        Oh, but for tonight's topic, what did you contrive?

ROXANE: If you see him in passing,
                    you won't give him the slightest clue?

CYRANO: I shall be silent as a Capuchin sleeping in his pew.

ROXANE: Tonight I shall say

"Christian, I give you no topic at all.
Extemporize! Speak to me of love. Let the words simply fall!"

CYRANO *(smiling)*: Good!

ROXANE: "Good"? Why?

CYRANO: That is, Good-*Bye*
   as you best get ready.

ROXANE: Yes! *(She goes in. But before closing
          the door)* But *he* must have no chance to prepare.

CYRANO: Even if I were to see him, is it any of my affair?

*(She enters the house with her Duenna. Cyrano waits, then
crosses to the side of the stage opposite that at which de
Guiche exited. He looks both ways, then whistles.)*

CYRANO *(whispering)*:   Christian! Come!

CHRISTIAN *(appearing)*:   I'm nearly numb.
                        That was an eternity!

CYRANO: Nevermind.
           There is still abundant time to learn pretty
   much all you need to make Roxane swoon at your oratory.
   I know tonight's theme, so now for your lesson – a priori!

CHRISTIAN: No.

CYRANO: What?

CHRISTIAN: Tonight I shall woo Roxane
                  in my very own speech.

CYRANO: Really, Christian,
            I feel I may yet have a bit more to teach.

CHRISTIAN: No, I say!
                I'm troubled that all I give to Roxane I take
firstly from you. My letters, my words, in a sense, are all fake.

CYRANO: Chris –

CHRISTIAN: Cyrano, it was all fine and good at the start,
    but now that Roxane loves me I must play my own part.

CYRANO: But –

CHRISTIAN: Your lessons have been useful,
                                    I'm the first to admit
    it.   Indeed, you have taught me so much that now I feel fit
to persist in wooing Roxane with my very own charms.
    (Adamantly) If naught else,
                I know how to take a woman in my arms!

ROXANE *(at her balcony)*: Is that you, Christian?

(She returns into the house.)

CYRANO *(quietly to Christian)*: Speak for yourself then.
                                No more my protégé.

(He bows and exits.)

CHRISTIAN *(suddenly getting cold feet)*: No! Wait!
                                Cyrano! Stay!

(But he is gone.)

ROXANE (*entering from the front door*
  of her house): Christian, come sit beside me.
                              Why is it that you stand so far away?
(*He sits on the bench with her. Silence. Both*
  simultaneously take a deep breath.) How fragrant
the evening air. And such a moon! The night is bright as day.
    (*Another brief silence.*) So, now you must feed me
                              words of love. I will devour all you say.

  (*She closes her eyes.*)

CHRISTIAN (*after yet another silence*): I love you.

ROXANE: Go on.

CHRISTIAN: I love you.

ROXANE: Yes, you have your theme. Now do segue.
                    Embroider it as such.

CHRISTIAN: I love you...very much.

ROXANE: I ask for cream
        and all that you give me are the skimmings of milk?
  Embroidery, Christian!
                Turn those words of yours into threads of silk.
    How do you love me?

CHRISTIAN: How? Well. So very, very...*very* much.
  (*Moving close to her, impulsively*) May I kiss your neck?!

ROXANE (*rising*): Christian!

CHRISTIAN: Sorry! (*Desperately*) Then instead just a touch?
  I love you!

ROXANE: Oh, fine. Now we are right back where we started!

CHRISTIAN: No! - I do *not* love you!

ROXANE *(sitting back down)*: Better. At least you've departed
  from your theme.

CHRISTIAN: I *adore* you!

ROXANE *(as clouds obscure the moon, darkening
    the stage)*: And I may scream if you don't stop this soon!
  What is wrong, Christian?
 Your thoughts seem clouded, even more so than this moon?
And if your words, like that shrouded sphere, have lost their light
              I do fear my heart darkening no less than this night.

CHRISTIAN: I know.
  I just love you so, my mind's turned all…juggly.

ROXANE: Which displeases me more
                        than were you to turn ugly.
        So quickly gather your thoughts and become erudite.

CHRISTIAN: Roxane…I love –

ROXANE: Yes, I know. You love me. Well, Goodnight.

  (She goes to the door.)

CHRISTIAN *(pursuing her)*: You're going? But wait!
                    Roxane, please! I only meant to say –

ROXANE: That you *adore* me.
                  Yes, I know that too. Now, go away.

(She slams the door behind her. Cyrano applauds.)

CYRANO *(returning)*:   A great success.

CHRISTIAN: Oh, what a mess.
  Cyrano, help me!

CYRANO: Not I.

CHRISTIAN: But you must! Or I shall die,
                          right here beneath this tree.

(He falls prostrate face-down beneath the tree.)

CYRANO: Now, now; think more clearly.
  What of Roxane? How pleasantly would it surprise her
        come the morning, to find you here as fertilizer?

CHRISTIAN *(rising, grabbing him)*: Cyrano, please!
                          It's now or never to win back her love!

CYRANO *(gingerly removing Christian's hands)*: Perhaps
                it's so, Christian, that push at last has come to shove.
  I'll help you. Still, I don't see how –

(A light appears in Roxane's window.)

CHRISTIAN: Look!

CYRANO *(moved)*:   Her window.

CHRISTIAN *(loudly)*:   I *shall* die!!

CYRANO *(hushing him)*: Well, do so softly.
  (Scheming) Hmm, there is scant little light left in the sky.

CHRISTIAN: Yes?

CYRANO: In such darkness
     I think there is something to be done.

CHRISTIAN: Yes?!

CYRANO: Not that you deserve this,
          but Roxane may yet me won.

CHRISTIAN: Grand! And the plan?

CYRANO: You, stand there – there – before the balcony,
  while I hide beneath it, obscured by darkness and this tree.
    From that spot, I shall whisper everything you need to say.

CHRISTIAN: But Cyrano,
               I am afraid that she may hear – she may –

CYRANO: Quiet!

The PAGES *(entering with their instruments)*: Sir!

CYRANO: Their timing is impeccable; I can't deny it.
  (To the pages) Montfleury?

PAGE 1: Ran screaming!

PAGE 2:   If you want us to give chase…

BOTH PAGES: …we'll try it.

CYRANO: No, listen instead.
  I will have the two of you guard the ingress to this street.

BOTH PAGES: And?

CYRANO: If a man approaches play a sad song.
                              If a woman – something upbeat.

*(They salute and exit with a comical bit of business,
 perhaps in deciding who goes which way. Cyrano
 plants Christian in his place and then hides in the
 alcove. There he whispers to Christian.)*

                         Call her!

CHRISTIAN: Roxane!

ROXANE: Who is calling?

CHRISTIAN: I.

ROXANE: Who?

CHRISTIAN: Christian.

ROXANE: Oh, you again?
    Be gone. I am going in.

CHRISTIAN: No! Please. Give me a chance to explain.

CYRANO *(quietly)*: That's good. With feeling!

ROXANE: Why? You do not love me anymore.

*(Cyrano now mouths words for Christian while
 simultaneously performing a sort of sign-language
 game of Charades with those words.)*

CHRISTIAN *(following Cyrano's lead,*
  hesitantly and with many pauses): No...*ever*more!
      And more than mere...words...ever could...implore.

ROXANE: Better.

CHRISTIAN *(with the same business)*: Love...struggles as
              it..grows, as though an angry...infant
  whose...whose...bursts of temper...break the...cradle? -
              cradl*ing* heart, and shan't
    be willed away.

ROXANE: Better still, I say.
            But then what to do with such a child?

CHRISTIAN: What can be done with one so *itchy*? No!
          ...*Tickled*?...Uh, *raving mad*? ...Oh, *WILD!*

ROXANE: Christian?

CHRISTIAN: So *wild* and strong –
          already at...birth – a...Hercules!

ROXANE: Do continue, Christian.
        Once again your words begin to please.

CHRISTIAN: Strong enough new-born,
            to...strangle those twin snakes – Pride and...
  *(He struggles to interpret both Cyrano's mouthing of
  the word "Doubt" and the accompanying shrugs
  Cyrano use to help convey the term.)* and..and..and...
Pride and...*(An emphatic whisper)* Cyrano, I don't understand!
  *(Cyrano responds with a grossly exaggerated shrug.
  Christian misreads this and momentarily loses his
  head, screaming to Cyrano)* You don't know?!

ROXANE *(a bit taken aback)*: Would you have me guess?

CHRISTIAN *(repeating Cyrano's reply to him)*: "No?"
  (Then to Roxane) Yes! No! *(Finally, after Cyrano loudly
  whispers it)* "Doubt?" *(Cyrano acknowledges this, perhaps
  by tapping the end of his nose, as if to say, a la Charades,
                    "On the nose.")* Doubt! Pride and DOUBT!

ROXANE: Well said.
  But why speak in this manner so drawn-out and roundabout?

CYRANO *(pulling Christian into the alcove under the
  balcony, perhaps trading hats, and whispering)*: This
  is too complicated!

ROXANE *(as Cyrano steps out)*: Your words
                              hesitate tonight. Why?

CYRANO *(imitating Christian)*: Each gropes its way
                    in darkness toward the light of you on high.

ROXANE: My words have no such trouble.

CYRANO: My heart is open wide,
  too large a mark to miss. Yours may yet need to be pried
    open fully. Besides, your words descend; mine must climb,
        and whereas falling is swift, ascending does take time.

ROXANE: Yet even now how your alacrity does intensify.
  Instead of arduously climbing, your words begin to fly.

CYRANO: Yes, for as you have come to welcome them,
                        they have found their wings.

ROXANE: Still, you seem so far away.

CYRANO: And you so above, your speech brings
with it a danger most assured.

ROXANE: How so?

CYRANO: Let fall but one hard word -
one - and it will crush me as readily as if I were a feather.

ROXANE: I am coming down.
I see now that words are but a fragile tether.

*(She turns and enters her room. Cyrano
and Christian run towards each other.)*

CYRANO & CHRISTIAN *(loudly)*: No!

CHRISTIAN *(in a frantic whisper)*: Comes Roxane...

CYRANO *(similarly)*:   ...so goes our plan!

*(They run back to their respective places just as Roxane
returns to her balcony, having heard only the "No!")*

ROXANE: "No"? Then, Christian,
you must draw near to me. Here, stand on the bench.

CYRANO: No!

ROXANE: "No," again?! And why so great a "No?"

CYRANO: Because it would wrench
my heart to spoil this precious moment – my one chance
to speak to you in a most fateful circumstance –
Unseen!

ROXANE: Unseen?

CYRANO: Yes! While now in this moon-veiled black night
                I look heavenward and see a summer gown of white,
           you look down and see only the darkness of my cloak.
     Oh, Roxane, what bright promise this evening does invoke!
                You glean all light above; I garner but shadow below.
     Just how much this moment means to me, you can never know.

ROXANE: Then tell me.

CYRANO: If only I had the eloquence, the art –

ROXANE: But you do.

CYRANO: Tonight perhaps, for I speak from my heart
      as though for the first time.

ROXANE: Yes, even your voice seems new.

CYRANO: I have another voice tonight –
                     my own, to speak to you
                as myself, without the least fear of your mockery,
           scorn, or of you finding me some laughing-stock.

ROXANE: Worry
                     not of that. It is wholly inconceivable.

CYRANO: Still, allow me this chance, so irretrievable,
      to be so daring.

ROXANE: Why daring?

CYRANO: Because what am I,
      or any man that he *dare* ask for you? Which is why

I have hidden my heart behind words eloquent and neat
    and finally – unworthy.

ROXANE: But those words, are they not sweet?

CYRANO: Oh, Roxane,
                    not enough sweet for you and me tonight!

ROXANE: You have never spoken to me like this before.

CYRANO: Might
    I suggest there comes a moment perhaps once before we die
    - and heaven help all of those
                            who choose to pass that moment by -
        when a love of such utter profundity arises
    in the heart, that the prettiest word trivializes
        all, and even those sweet as honey carry a bee's sting.

ROXANE: And if this moment has come
                            to you and me, then what thing
    is there left to say? And what words to say it?

CYRANO: Every! All!
All the words that blossom in my heart, and from my lips fall
    in wild profusion at your feet. Love? I am choked with love.
            I love beyond breath, beyond reason, beyond and above
love's own limits! Your name rings like a bell within my heart:
            "Roxane." I tremble at its tolling. There is not a part
of a single day forgotten so long as you were there to share
    it. On the twelfth of May
                    you changed a bit the way you wore your hair -
    Such hair! It is like a light upon my eyes, and one
    n'er overshadowed by moon, nor even noonday sun.
            And, as it is when we give that sun a prolonged glance,
                one look at you, and I am blinded by your radiance.

ROXANE: Yes...that is...love.

CYRANO: Yes. And for your happiness,
                 I would surrender my own.
 Only tonight – this splendid night –
         do I dare say these things, I to you alone,
 and you hear them, Roxane! It is my voice, my own, mine
         that makes you tremble as a leaf blown about its vine.

ROXANE: Yes, I tremble. And I weep. And I do love you. Oh,
 I am yours, and you have made me thus.

CYRANO: Can it be so?
  It is more than I have ever dreamed. That I have done this,
  myself. Then only let me ask for one more thing –

CHRISTIAN: A kiss!

ROXANE *(taken aback)*: What?

CYRANO: ...Oh, God.

ROXANE: You ask –

CYRANO: Yes, but - *(Whispering to Christian)*
                 Christian, you go too fast!

CHRISTIAN *(whispering back)*: No, Cyrano,
               you have shaken her; the die is cast!

CYRANO *(to Roxane)*: Yes, I do ask, Roxane,
            but I know that I do ask *too much.*

ROXANE: Just one? That's all; no more?

CHRISTIAN *(uncontrollably letting escape*
  a loud gasp of a sigh): Oh!

CYRANO *(hitting him)*: Truly, I offend you with such
                                   impetuosity. So I ask you to refuse.

CHRISTIAN *(whispered)*: What?! But why? Why?
                                   Cyrano, what have we got to lose?

CYRANO: Christian, will you shut-up!

ROXANE: Christian, what is that you say?

CYRANO: I am angry and ashamed at my imprudent way
  so I tell myself *(to Christian)* "Christian, shut-up!"
                                   Too soon, too soon.
  (The theorbos begin to play.) Hark! Someone is coming.
                    (Roxane retreats inside.) Both a sad *and* happy tune?
            Is it man or woman? Or are my pages simply drunk?
    (Noticing offstage) Ah, that explains the strange duet –
                                   it's a Capuchin *Monk*!
                    (The monk enters carrying a lantern.)
                    Ah, Priest. Why this promenade ala Diogenes?

CAPUCHIN: I seek the home of Madeleine Robin, if you please.

CHRISTIAN *(pointing off)*: That way.
  Keep moving forward. You will find it over there.

CAPUCHIN: Bless you, sir.
                    Be assured you shall be in my next prayer.

CYRANO *(to Christian as the monk exits up*
  one aisle of the audience): He may be lost, but not remiss.

CHRISTIAN: Now, Cyrano, win me that kiss!

CYRANO: No!

CHRISTIAN: Sooner or later –

CYRANO: it must happen. …That is so.

ROXANE *(re-entering the balcony)*: Christian, are you still
    there? *(Christian hides.)* You were speaking of…you know.

CYRANO: Of a kiss. Are your lips afraid even of its name?
No need. A gentle word – and deed, not cause for fear or shame.

ROXANE: Hush.

CYRANO: And then, what is a kiss when all is said and done?
                    The seal fixed upon a promise given one to one,
a moment made immortal with a rush of unseen wings,
a new song to an old and simple tune, that one heart sings
                    to another, and a sacrament of blossoms, too.

ROXANE: Come! Gather your sacred blossoms…

CYRANO *(to Christian)*: Go!

CHRISTIAN: Who, me?

CYRANO: Yes, you!

ROXANE: Come here to me, my love,
                    and let your heart sing that old new song…

CYRANO: Go on!

CHRISTIAN *(hesitating)*: Now that the moment's come,
                         I can't help wonder if it's wrong.

ROXANE: Come fix your seal upon this promise.

CYRANO: Go, you fool!

*(Christian grabs one of the two long drapes hanging to
the ground, intending to use it to help him scale the wall.
His sturdy tug tears it from the high window, landing him
flat on his back, the yards of material dropping on top of
him. Cyrano nonchalantly opens the door for him, and
signals him to use it. He does so.)*

CHRISTIAN *(entering the balcony)*: Roxane.

*(He takes her in his arms and kisses her. She leads him
back inside.)*

CYRANO *(to himself)*:   A strange weight
is the heart, for its size ungodly heavy. …And so this is my fate:
     To stand - another Lazarus - outside the *lovers'* feast,
       handed only the slightest crumb of comfort, but at least
         one that I will savor:
                         That in this most bittersweet of partnerships,
                 it is my words this night that she is kissing –
                                 my words – upon his lips.

*(Standing alone in the moonlight, he smiles. But the smile
soon fades from his face, as music begins again. It's the two
theorbos [or whatever] playing again – one a sad, the other
a happy tune, as before. These pieces complement each other
and perfectly reflect Cyrano's ambivalence. As the curtain
falls, there is a build of instrumentation, a richly orches-*

trated rendering of the two merged pieces playing into the
***Intermission**.)*

End of Act I

(NOTE: Should it serve a production to place the Intermis-
sion at the end of a different scene, or even to provide two
Intermissions, then Act I, Scene iii and Act II, Scene i can
simply be merged under the single title "Roxane's Kiss.")

Act II

Scene i: Hardly A Honey*moon*

(As the house lights fade, the same music that closed Act I begins again with its full orchestration. At the curtain's rise, the instruments start dropping out so that at full-rise and lights-up, only the two off-stage theorbos are left playing their contrasting tunes. Cyrano is found exactly as we left him.)

CYRANO: A sad tune. A merry tune. The monk is back again! *(Pretending to have run from a distance, he calls)* Hello!

ROXANE *(entering the balcony)*: Who is it?

CYRANO: It is I. Have you seen Christian?

CHRISTIAN *(entering the balcony)*: Cyrano!?!

ROXANE: What brings you nigh, sir?

CYRANO: A caller, good cousin.

ROXANE: I'll come right down.

(She exits the balcony.)

CYRANO *(to Christian)*: You best come too. It's the Capuchin.

140

(Christian exits the balcony. The Capuchin Monk arrives on stage down the opposite aisle from which he entered the audience in Act I, Scene iii. He may have been searching there for Roxane's house since near the end of the Intermission.)

CAPUCHIN: She *does* live here. So I am told.

CYRANO: Who?

CAPUCHIN: Madeleine Robin.

CYRANO: Well, she had better. It's her home.

ROXANE *(entering with Christian through the front door, to a confused monk)*: Please, friar, do come in.

CAPUCHIN: No need. I am only to deliver this letter to you
(*-he does so-)* from an excellent Lord –
                    I quote – both "noble and *well-to-do*."

ROXANE *(to Christian)*: De Guiche.

CHRISTIAN: He dares?

CYRANO: And dares provide his own – quote – "biography."
    (And leading the monk away) Good friar,
                    might we discuss a question of theology
    while you await Mademoiselle Robin's eager reply?

ROXANE *(reading to Christian)*: "Roxane,
            in spite of your words, I remain on the sly
            at this Abbey, as my battalion prepares to depart.
    The drums are beating, but not as loudly as does my heart.

I shall arrive disguised tonight when all the world's asleep.
Fear not; our secret's safe; this monk's as simple as a sheep."

CHRISTIAN: And if de Guiche tries to play the ram,
                              I'll make him a ewe!

ROXANE: Wait. *(To the Capuchin)*: Friar!
      This letter is of concern to you. *(To Christian)* You, too.
                  (Cyrano and the monk gather around her.)
      Listen. You must hear this, though the news is most distressing.
                  (She pretends to read.)
      "Dear Mademoiselle, the Cardinal sends to you his blessing,
      but insists on having his way in opposing your desire.
      That is why I have sent this particularly wise friar –
            the most saintly, reliable, and discreet of holy men –
      whom I order to perform your sacred matrimony - "

CAPUCHIN: Where? When?

ROXANE: "Here and at once between you and…"
                              Oh, with grief I am beset!

CAPUCHIN: Courage, my child.

ROXANE: "between you and…and…Christian de Neuvillette."

CYRANO: Yes, courage, cousin.

ROXANE: "Now, you must overcome your repugnance
      for this be the will and the command of His Eminence."
      Signed, Your Very Humble et cetera, et cetera, et cetera.
                              (Melodramatically) Oh, dear!

CAPUCHIN *(turning the light of his lantern
      on Cyrano)*: So you are the –

CHRISTIAN: No, the groom is me!

*(The monk turns his light on Christian, and
becomes immediately suspicious at the sight
of such a handsome face.)*

CAPUCHIN: So ripe a peach.
                      Hmmm, something *smells* funny, I fear.

ROXANE: Wait, there's a postscript!
                      "Give the Abbey in my name
a hundred *(- Cyrano indicates 'higher' to her-)*
                      and twenty pistoles." *Signed* – the same.

CAPUCHIN: Resign yourself, my child!

ROXANE *(martyred)*: I shall!

CYRANO *(sniffing the air)*: Magically gone.

CHRISTIAN: What?

CYRANO: That *smell*.

ROXANE *(handing Cyrano the letter)*: So,
 what do you think, Cyrano; did I not read the letter well?

 (A single theorbos plays – sad music.)

CYRANO: Sad music. That denotes…de Guiche.

CHRISTIAN: The cad. He's on his way.

ROXANE: Please, dearest Cyrano,
                      you must somehow keep him at bay!

CYRANO *(to the monk)*: How much time
  do you need to perform the marriage vows?

CAPUCHIN: Well, I've
  done so in as little as fifteen minutes, but –

CYRANO: You've got five!
  (Calling off) Pages!

PAGES *(entering on the run)*: Sir?

CYRANO: I want you to stick to the heels of this good friar.

PAGES: Yes, sir!

  (They instantly converge on the monk.)

CYRANO: When the work he's to do is completed, then I require
  that you play a suitable tune loud enough for me to hear,
          while I see to it that our visitor does not interfere.
  Now, hurry! *(He hustles everyone into the house.)*
                      I've an idea. Nevertheless, you must not tarry.
  (They all exit into the house.)
        Actually, I've not a clue…Nor any want to see her marry
    another. Still, for her happiness I best act soon.
  (The moon comes out, giving Cyrano a plan.)
    Ah, shining friend; your arrival is most opportune.
                      First, I will need to hide
  this unique and ample…face *(- which he does
  beneath his hat and that drape Christian tore down)*.
                                      And then disguise my voice
  (- doing so -) like so! Who knows?
        In this antic masquerade I may even somewhat rejoice.

(He crumples to the ground and lies very still.
A masked de Guiche enters groping about.)

DE GUICHE: This damn mask may have been a mistake;
                                    I can barely see.

(He is startled upon stumbling atop of Cyrano
who lets out a huge moan.) Is that you, fool Capuchin?
                                    Wake-up immediately!

CYRANO: Do be gentle, sir, I have fallen, you know,
                                    quite like a brick.

DE GUICHE *(looking up, puzzled)*: From where?

CYRANO *(pointing up)*: There.

DE GUICHE: Where?

CYRANO: Why, the moon; where else?

DE GUICHE: The man's a lunatic.

(He attempts to pass Cyrano who rises and
staggers into his arms.)

CYRANO: Thank you, kind sir,
  I'm afraid I'm still a little shaky from my plummet
  off yon silver sphere.

DE GUICHE: If you say so.

CYRANO: I do! But, oh, I am not from it.

DE GUICHE: Of course not.

CYRANO: I am from Earth.

DE GUICHE: Hard to believe. Now, if you are through –

*(Cyrano lets out a sudden cry, which yet
again causes de Guiche to recoil.)*

CYRANO: But what strange world is this
on which I've spilled?!   Your face – your face – it's blue!

DE GUICHE: What are you raving about?
                    (Remembering) Oh, this. Calm down; it's just a mask.

CYRANO: Have I landed then in Venice – or Genoa - may I ask?

DE GUICHE: A lady is waiting, if you must know.
                                        So please stop your rants –

CYRANO *(cutting him off)*: "A lady is waiting," you say?
                                Ah, then this must be Paris, France.

DE GUICHE *(smiling in spite of himself)*: This fool
becomes amusing.

CYRANO: Ah! You laugh? …Or is that just gas?

DE GUICHE: You are a witty madman,
                            but now do kindly let me pass.

*(He tries to push past, but Cyrano thrusts
out a leg, tripping de Guiche.)*

CYRANO: See this tooth stuck in my boot;
                            I was nipped by Ursa, the Big Bear.
Fleeing him, I barely dodged the Scorpion's deadly derriere.

Navigating past Aquarius, I got all "mal de mer,"
and when Orion belted me, why, I saw stars everywhere!
I tell you, after being up there betwixt each constellation,
returning safely back to Earth is no small consolation
for my – *(De Guiche makes a sudden move.*
Cyrano gets in his way.) Careful! Strike my nose,
and out of it milk indubitably will spray.

DE GUICHE: Milk?

CYRANO: Of course. As you would expect,
on my way down, I passed right through the Milky Way.

DE GUICHE: Really, –

CYRANO *(interrupting again)*: When I write my book,
I shall divulge all of these great risks,
and these little stars I shake from my cloak,
I'll save for asterisks.

DE GUICHE: Enough! I wish –

CYRANO: I know! You wish to learn how, in the first place,
I devised a way to carry myself into outer space.
The moon can be reached
by at least three techniques I have invented.

DE GUICHE: Move aside, loon,
I am not interested in your demented –

CYRANO: As an instance: Stripping myself as naked as a baby,
I splash on daybreak's dew.
"How much?" Oh, several liters maybe.
Then for the heat of the morning sun I need only await
in order to rise with the dew as it does evaporate.

DE GUICHE *(a bit intrigued)*:   Well, all right, yes; that's one.

CYRANO: Oh, but I've just begun!
  Here, picture this: I construct a mechanical grasshopper,
    its spring-operated legs fueled by the precisely proper
  amount of salt-peter, loaded – most cautiously - into the works.
    Then, astride, I *hop* to the moon! –
                        though, I allow, in fits and jerks.

DE GUICHE: Well, that's two, and rather smart of you.

CYRANO: Merci beaucoup.
  But may I present my true breakthrough?

DE GUICHE: By all means, do.

CYRANO: Last, but not least,
            seating myself on an iron plate, I throw
  a gigantic magnet into the air. Then it's up I go! –
  the plate pulled after. I catch the magnet and throw it again,
            and so proceed, ad infinitum, to the lunar domain.

DE GUICHE: The third. And the best yet that I've heard.
            So, which one of these three means did you use?

CYRANO: Why, none!

DE GUICHE: Then how?

CYRANO: You'll just have to guess.

DE GUICHE: You can't be serious!

CYRANO: All right, some clues.

*(Reluctantly, Cyrano imitates the sound of
waves with his voice, and mimics their motions
with outlandish gestures.)*

DE GUICHE: Uh..uh..hmm...Um.
    (Giving up) I'm afraid I haven't the slightest notion.

CYRANO *(to self)*: And he finds me the idiot.
                (To de Guiche) It's the Atlantic Ocean!
When the hour approached for the full moon to draw its tide
    I serenely bobbed on the waves and enjoyed my ride.

DE GUICHE: A brain*storm*!

CYRANO: Well, anyway - wet!

DE GUICHE: Yes, quite naturally –

*(A celebratory song begins inside the
house, played on the theorbos.)*

CYRANO: And yet...

DE GUICHE: And yet?

CYRANO: My friend,
    you must prepare yourself for a very great shock.

DE GUICHE: Shock?

CYRANO *(in his normal voice)*: Our time's up,
  you're free to pass, for they are now bound – in holy wedlock.

DE GUICHE: That voice!
  (The door of the house opens. The Capuchin enters

*with his lantern, followed by the two performing
pages and the Duenna in her nightclothes. Cyrano
removes his hat. De Guiche sees his face at last.)*
                                                      That nose!

CYRANO *(saluting)*:   What, no "hellos"
  for the newlyweds?

DE GUICHE: What?

  *(Christian and Roxane appear from the house,
  entering hand in hand.)*

CYRANO: United today…*(with a change of tone)* and forever.

ROXANE: Thank you, cousin.

DE GUICHE *(bowing to Roxane)*: Congratulations, dear.
                          You've been quite clever.
  (To Cyrano) And my compliments to you, sir.
            (To others) The pictures this man paints
  of such masterful invention would even give the Saints
    themselves cause for pause
               on their heavenly ascension. Sir, to you I say
  you must not fail to write that book
               with all its starry asterisks one day.

CYRANO *(bowing)*: Thank you, Comte de Guiche.
                   I shall heed your advice.

DE GUICHE: And I shall buy a copy.

CYRANO: For you – half-price.

DE GUICHE *(turning on the pages)*: Will you two
                              cease that confounded folderol!

(They stop playing.)

CYRANO: Thank you, my pages pro tem. That will be all.

(They bolt.)

DUENNA: But look at Monsieur et Madame.
                              Aren't they a handsome pair.

CAPUCHIN: Yes, and joined together by God –
                              and that good man over there
          (indicating de Guiche, who smiles...coldly).

DE GUICHE: Together, yes, good friar,
                    But, alas, I'm afraid not for long.

CAPUCHIN: I do not understand.

CHRISTIAN: Too late, de Guiche.
                    The priest did nothing wrong.

DE GUICHE: You mistake my meaning.
              Still, say Goodbye to your lovely bride.
     The Cadets leave tonight.

CYRANO: For the front?

(De Guiche nods.)

ROXANE *(quietly)*:   But our plan?

DE GUICHE: Nullified.

(Producing the dispatch) Here is the order.
            (To Christian) Deliver this to your division now.
*(Roxane throws herself into Christian's arms. De Guiche
continues to Cyrano)* It seems the wedding night must wait.

CYRANO *(to self)*:   I'm not too distraught somehow.

CHRISTIAN *(to Roxane)*: Your lips again…

DE GUICHE: Enough of that!

CYRANO *(to Christian)*: Come.

CHRISTIAN *(still holding Roxane)*: You can't
                            know how difficult –

CYRANO: Oh, but I do.

*(The beating of drums is heard in
the distance.)*

DE GUICHE: The battalion is on the move!

CAPUCHIN *(practically collapsing
            into the arms of the Duenna)*: Oh, such tumult!

DE GUICHE: Forward march, soldier. Immediately!

*(Roxane runs to her groom and holds tight.
Christian takes one last look at her and runs
off, dispatch in hand. De Guiche starts to
follow, stops, and hauls the Capuchin off with
him. Roxane grabs Cyrano who has also
begun to follow.)*

ROXANE: Please, Cyrano, take care of him for me.
          Keep him out of danger, promise me this!

CYRANO: Roxane, I will try, but I can't promise.

ROXANE: Make him be careful.

CYRANO: I'll try.

ROXANE: See that he keeps warm and dry.

CYRANO: In war? Well, if it is possible…

ROXANE: And promise he will remain faithful.

CYRANO *(taking her hands)*: My dear Roxane –
          Madame – I am certain Christian would never forsake –

ROXANE: Oh, but see that he writes often!

*(She squeezes his hands and then runs
weeping into the house in the arms of
her Duenna.)*

CYRANO: Now, *that* is a promise I can make!

*(The drums grow deafeningly loud as the
lights fade quickly to black.)*

Scene ii: The Siege Of Arras

*(The military tattoo is punctuated now and again by the
sound of an explosion accompanied by its flash of light.*

These flashes illuminate the scene change that is carried out
by the Cadets who duck and cringe at each near miss. At the
completion of the change, a rampart or battlement traverses
the entire upstage plane. Drapery forms a tent or two
downstage of this. There are scattered weapons, drums, etc. A
few campfires dot the landscape, and the Cadets sleep hud-
dled around them, wrapped tightly in their cloaks. The drums
fade as the light gradually rises. Day is breaking at the siege
of Arras.)

LE BRET *(softly muttering to himself)*: What irony!
          To have our siege besieged. No, not irony – a disaster!
     To die from a bullet would be far more preferable

                              and so much faster
          than this wretched and unending deprivation.
     To fight, not starve, is a soldier's true vocation.
     (Gunfire erupts not too far away. Some of the Cadets stir.)
     Curse that musketry!
          Hmpf. I could sleep through it too when I was younger.
               (More shots and more stirring.)
          I hope they do sleep yet awhile.

                              It is their sole relief from hunger.

CADET 7 *(sitting up)*: What is it?

LE BRET: Hush, boy. Get your sleep.

                              It's only Cyrano coming back.

(The Cadet lies down again.)

OFFSTAGE VOICE OF SENTRY: Halt! Who goes there?

OFFSTAGE VOICE OF CYRANO: Well,
          who does it look like, fool? It's me – De Bergerac.

(Cyrano enters over the rampart. Le Bret nervously crosses to him.)

LE BRET: Are you wounded?

CYRANO *(indicating the sleeping Cadets)*: Shh.
    Nary a scratch. It has become their habit to miss me.

LE BRET: Still, to steal about before each sunrise
                seems plain stupid and far too risky -
            and all for the sake of a letter!

CYRANO: My dear Le Bret, you know me better
    than to think for a moment
             that I would not keep a promise without fail.
   I promised that he would write often.
                  To not go would be a betrayal
   of them both. And look at Christian –
         still handsome while starving to death.
   No, I will risk my life to make the mail
              unto my own last breath,
which may draw much sooner than any of us would expect.

LE BRET: You've seen something?

CYRANO: I'll tell you later, once I've double-checked.

LE BRET: Get some sleep!

CYRANO *(affectionately)*: Stop growling, Le Bret.

LE BRET: All for a letter. Holy Mother
   of God! *(Cyrano crosses to a tent.)*
 Now, where are you going?

CYRANO: Where else, my friend, to write another.

(He enters the tent. Distant cannon fire sounds,
followed by a trumpet or roll of drums. The
voices of officers are heard far off.)

LE BRET: Already reveille?
  Seems the devil will see
    my boys get no food – or rest!

(The Cadets have begun to rouse
themselves, stretching, etc.)

CADET 1: Dawn so soon?

CADET 2:   I can hardly sleep
  anymore, my stomach grumbles so loud.

CADET 3:   I know! Must it keep
  the rest of us awake, too?

CADET 4: I'd trade my coronet for one slice of cheese.

LE BRET: No appetite for war, men?
          Would you sulk in your tents – like Achilles?

ALL: Yes!

LE BRET: And what then of your sense of duty
              and the pride of our brigade?

CADET 7: Go ask that of the Spaniards
      who have us penned in their damned blockade.

CADET 1: We've grown wholly *fed* up of this stranglehold!

CADET 2: Please. Don't say "fed!"

LE BRET: Enough! Such complaints grow old!
    (Calling) Cyrano!

CADET 3: Our complaints may well grow old; we won't.
                    What choice have we but to die…

CADET 4: …Or desert.

ALL: "Dessert?!"

*(They clutch their stomachs and moan as Cyrano
enters from the tent, pen and paper in hand.)*

CYRANO: You called, Le Bret?

LE BRET: Cheer them up. You're better at it than I.

CADET 5 *(to 6 who is hiding something)*: Hey,
    what's that you're eating?

CADET 6:   Gun wads with axle-grease. Want a bite?

*(He pushes it in 5's face. They go at each
other until Cyrano and Le Bret separate them.)*

CYRANO: Wrong battle, my brother Gascons.
                    It's the Spaniards we must fight.

CADET 7: Easier said than done
                    with our bellies hollow as a drum.

CYRANO: Then let's beat the long roll on them,
                    and prove what stock we're from.

CADET 1: Always the clever answer.

CYRANO: The better to drive home the point
    that here we do a grand thing for a good cause. Best we anoint
    ourselves in glory – dying in battle, not in a fevered bed.

LE BRET: Your words nourish the soul –

CADET 7 *(crossing to the rampart)*: I'd prefer they
                            fill the stomach instead.

   (Murmurs.)

CYRANO: Can not even one of you think of anything
                                besides eating?

CADET 2: We're hungry!

CADET 3:   Famished!

CADET 4:   Starving!

CYRANO: Such belly-aching's self-defeating.
    You there *(- Cadet 5 -),*

                    weren't you a shepherd back home in Gascony?
    (5 nods.) Then bring out your fife and play us a gentle melody
    that harkens back to halcyon days in our dear beloved South.
    Playing the pipe – What better way to occupy an idle mouth?

   *(The Cadet begins to play a sad Provencal tune. He is soon
   joined by Cadet 6 on a lute, guitar, or other such instrument.
   Before long one Cadet begins singing, breaking the others'*

hearts with his angelic voice. All soon join in. When the
song is over, there is a profound silence, heads are bowed,
and some of the men furtively brush away tears.)

CYRANO *(as Cadet 5 plays a coda)*: Listen, Gascons.
   That is not the shrill fife of the soldier's camp
                                           upon those lips;
   rather the gentle flute of a much beloved woodland
                                           that never slips
   from memory. Listen! That is the forest, the dale, the heath,
   and the beckoning hearth, too!
                  It is the green sweetness of nights beneath
   our lofty, deep-rooted pines.
        It is a sound rich and pungent as our native loam.
   Oh, listen, you Gascons: It is all of Gascony!
                              All of family! …All home.

LE BRET *(softly to Cyrano)*:   I asked you to bring them cheer.
                              Now, on every face – a tear.

CYRANO: Homesickness is the much more noble
                                  hunger of the heart.
   It will help them forget their stomachs and to do their part
        on the battlefield. They will never yield to their agony
             when fighting in honor and in memory of Gascony.

LE BRET: I only hope, Cyrano, you are right.

CYRANO: I'll show you they are ready for a fight.
   (He gestures to Cadet 6. The Cadet sharply beats his
   drum. All the others spring up and rush for their weapons.)
             Look at that, Le Bret – you see – *all* of them, not some!
             What the fife lulls to rest is wakened by the drum.

(The sound of hoof-beats is heard approaching.)

OFFSTAGE VOICE OF SENTRY: The Colonel!

CADET 7 *(from the rampart)*:   Our infernal
          Comte de Guiche!

CYRANO: Here to teach
          us another lesson in proper conduct and of valor.

CADET 1: I'm sick of him.

CADET 2:   The preening peacock!

CADET 7 *(looking off)*:   He *is* looking paler.

CADET 3: Fact is, despite his finery, he is as hungry as anyone.

CADET 4: Yes, and with so many jewels on his belt,
                              his cramps glitter in the sun!

     (Laughter.)

CYRANO: You see, Le Bret.
     What did I tell you? Here is the Gascon heart bespoken!

LE BRET: That's it, boys!
     Don't give him the satisfaction of seeing our spirit broken!

     *(They all busy themselves with cards, dice, the lighting of
     clay pipes, etc. Cyrano – using the drum as a table, gets
     back to work on his letter.)*

DE GUICHE *(entering over the rampart)*: Good morning.
     (No response.) I said "Good morning!"

ALL *(like school children)*: Good morning, Comte de Guiche.

DE GUICHE: I know
that you hold your Colonel in disdain. But why? Because I show
  a dignity you label vain, and cloak my armor in some lace?
  Well, I can afford your contempt.
                              My accomplishments prove my place.
    Why, only yesterday
      I led a decisive charge against the Spanish force –
      a classic of military maneuvers.

CYRANO: And what of that white scarf of yours?

DE GUICHE: So that's already gotten 'round?
                              Well, what happened was this:
      Rallying my men, I was swept into a most dangerous
      situation, trapped behind enemy lines. So I thought quick,
      and flung away the white scarf marking my rank.
                                        That did the trick!
          Being thus inconspicuous, I escaped quite easily,
      Whereupon I soon returned, leading my troops to victory!

(There is no response from the Cadets.)

CYRANO: Sir, your courage is quite different
                              from that of a Cadet
  who would not surrender the honor of being a target.
  Were I there when your scarf fell, I should have run to put it on.

DE GUICHE: Ha!

CYRANO: Indeed, perhaps I will wear it when next we call upon
  the Spaniards.

DE GUICHE: An idle boast
                    as it is in a place no one could reach alive.

CYRANO: Ah, but you see, Colonel, I have it here
(- *he draws it from a pocket*), and the last I looked I did survive.

*(The Cadets stifle their laughter behind their cards and hats.
De Guiche looks at them and they immediately return to their
games, etc. One of them casually whistles the pastoral song
played earlier on the fife.)*

DE GUICHE *(taking the scarf)*: Thank you.
  A white scarf should make as fine a signal as can be.
  I was hesitating about this; now you've decided me.

*(He climbs the rampart and waves the scarf above
his head several times. This troubles the Cadets.)*

CADET 5: What's he "decided?"

CADET 6:　　　　　　A "signal" for what!?

CYRANO: Indubitably, some odious plot.

(A gunshot sounds.)

SENTRY *(his head appearing over the rampart,
to Le Bret)*: Sorry, sir. I missed him – a Spaniard running away.

DE GUICHE: Yes, my pet Spanish spy
　　　　　　　　　　　　whom I've long kept in our pay.
Gentlemen, I have been compelled to make a difficult decision.
    As you well know, our army is in dire need of reprovision.
  The Marshall has taken near our entire force to get supplies.
  My informants tell me the Spaniards are planning a surprise
      attack. My signal will bring it here with all its fire-power.
      *(The Cadets all rise and start buckling on swords,
  breastplates, etc.)* Gentlemen, you have perhaps an hour.

CADETS: Oh, well – an hour!

(They all unbuckle, sit down, and casually
resume their games, etc.)

DE GUICHE *(to Le Bret)*: The Marshall *will* return.
                    The main thing is to gain what time we can.

LE BRET: And your advice?

DE GUICHE: Kindly lay down your lives to the very last man.

CYRANO: And so your revenge.

DE GUICHE: I make no pretense of loving you.
    and whereas I could have made a different choice, it's true,
                who else is as courageous as the Cadets of Gascony?
    Therefore, while serving myself, I also serve King and country.

CYRANO *(saluting)*: Our thanks.

DE GUICHE *(saluting back)*: Besides,
                you just love to fight a hundred against one.
    So here's another chance, Cyrano, to have a little fun.
    (To Le Bret)   Now, let us bivouac, Captain
                    to review my battle plan.

LE BRET *(to a Cadet)*: Stand up, man!
                    Now, give me your back!

(Using the back of this Cadet as a table, they open a map.)

DE GUICHE: Here, Le Bret, my counterattack.

(They review the plan while Cyrano crosses to Christian, who has remained motionless through the above.)

CYRANO: Christian? *(He puts his hand on his shoulder.)*

CHRISTIAN *(shaking his head)*: How did the good priest
                        end our vows? "Til death do you part."
   ...I should dearly like you to consign all that is in my heart
to one final missive my Roxane might hold forever dear.

CYRANO: I thought such might be needed today,
                        Christian. I have it here.
   *(And handing Christian the letter he wrote over the
   course of the scene)* To...*your*...Roxane.

CHRISTIAN: My farewell letter?
   (Cyrano shrugs an affirmation.) Should I read it?

CYRANO: Perhaps you'd better.

   *(Christian unfolds the letter and begins to read it.
   He suddenly stops.)*

CHRISTIAN: My God.

CYRANO: What?

CHRISTIAN: This little circle.

CYRANO *(taking the letter back)*: A smudge of ink.

CHRISTIAN: A stain!

CYRANO: Well, what of it?

CHRISTIAN: What - ? Why, it's a teardrop; that's very plain.

CYRANO *(examining it)*: And so it is.
              You see, as a poet I must feel
          that all I am imagining is utterly real.
     Writing this note for you, my friend, away I was swept
        by feelings of such profound sentiment that –

CHRISTIAN: you wept?

CYRANO: Because,
           while it is of little enough consequence to die,
      to never ever see Roxane again is just more than *I* –
        (Christian looks at him) more than *we* -
                  (quickly) more than *YOU* –

CHRISTIAN *(snatching the letter)*: Give me that!

     *(He stuffs it into his shirt, between buttons,
     as the sound of a carriage approaches.)*

OFFSTAGE VOICE OF SENTRY *(shouting)*: Halt! I say Halt!

DE GUICHE: What's this?! So soon the enemy's assault?

LE BRET *(while dismissing the "map-table")*: Of that
                          I shall straight away inquire.

OFFSTAGE VOICE OF SENTRY *(still shouting)*: Halt,
                      driver! Halt now or I shall fire!

LE BRET *(re-entering the scene)*: What is it, Cadet?

CADET 7 *(on the rampart)*:   A carriage is approaching!

OFFSTAGE VOICE OF RAGUENEAU: Don't shoot,
				don't shoot! We come in service of the King!

CADET 7 *(to Le Bret, as with a jingle of the harness,*
  the carriage stops): The coachman seems familiar.

OFFSTAGE VOICE OF SENTRY: Then, driver,
						say who goes there!

		(Some offstage discussion impossible to make out.)

LE BRET: Sentry!

SENTRY *(his head appearing again)*: It's a coach, sir.
				Drove right through the enemy lines, I swear!
	Captain, the driver claims they have come here
					in the King's service.

DE GUICHE *(now re-entering the scene,*
  barking orders): Hats off to the Crown! Fall in!
	Bow down! Sound the drum! *(To Le Bret)* Did I miss
	anything?

		*(As Cadet 6 drums a tatoo, the others, having followed the
		above commands, bow low and wait as a hooded figure en-
		ters over the rampart.)*

ROXANE *(lowering her cowl)*: Why, good morning, gentlemen.
				How good it is to see you all again.

		*(At the sound of a woman's voice, every head raises.
		A sensation ensues.)*

DE GUICHE: The King's service?

ROXANE: My own King's.

                  I come the steward of Love's Majesty.

CYRANO: Oh, merciful heaven.

CHRISTIAN *(hastening to her)*: You are really here, Roxane.

                            How can it be?

ROXANE *(taking his hands)*: This war of yours

        has gone on far too long. I had to come.

CHRISTIAN: But - ?

ROXANE: Not now.

DE GUICHE: You cannot remain here.

ROXANE *(to Cadet 6)*:   Please, bring me your drum.
  (He does so.) Thank you. *(She sits down on it.)*
        But you see, Colonel de Guiche, of course I can.

CYRANO *(to self, having not turned to look at her)*: Steady,

             Cyrano. Do you dare look at her again?

ROXANE *(spotting him)*: Cousin, I am glad to see you!

CYRANO: Oh – Roxane. How ever –

ROXANE: - did I find you? It was not a difficult endeavor.
    I just followed the countryside that was laid to waste.

CYRANO: But through the enemy lines?

ROXANE: To every Spaniard faced,
  I simply reported: "I am on my way to see my lover!"

Each would bow low and say: "Pass Senorita."
     (All laugh except Christian.) I did discover
     curiously, that this ploy would not work as planned
      if instead of "lover," I used the word "husband."

    (More laughs.)

CHRISTIAN: But Roxane –

ROXANE: Oh, can you forgive me?

CHRISTIAN: Of course, but – you must leave here.

ROXANE: Why?

CYRANO: Because you may soon not find
  the Spaniards so polite.

ROXANE: Oh, dear,
  you are about to fight. Still, I will stay –

ALL *(pleading)*: No!

ROXANE *(throwing herself in Christian's arms)*: - at
                                Christian's side.

DE GUICHE *(desperate)*: Today this is a dangerous post.

LE BRET: And no place for a bride.

ROXANE: How dangerous?

CHRISTIAN: About the most.

CYRANO: The Colonel would have us finally earn our pay.

LE BRET: But not likely collect it.

ROXANE: So you wish, monsieur, to make a widow of me?

DE GUICHE: Pray
                    tell, Madame, I would not deceive –

ROXANE *(interrupting)*:   It matters not. I shall not leave.

CYRANO *(bowing)*:   Roxane, you are a true heroine.

ROXANE *(with a curtsey in return)*: I am, after all, your cousin.

CADET 1: Madame de Neuvillette, we will fight hard and fast -

CADET 2:   to defend and protect you to the very last.

   (Cadets chime in randomly: "Hear, hear!"…
   "Yes!" … "Indeed!" etc.)

ROXANE: I feel most safe with you, my friends.
                              Do you as well, Colonel?

DE GUICHE: Christian,
                do convince your wife to depart before all hell
breaks loose. Now, Cadets of Gascony,
I must take leave of you…to order the mustering of an
                                                   ordnance.

   (He exits.)

LE BRET: That's the last we'll see of him.

   (Roxane and Christian embrace.)

CYRANO *(gripping Le Bret)*: I can't look.

LE BRET: What?! *(Then realizing what his
  friend is talking about)* Come now,
                              you face death every day.

CYRANO: There I have a fighting chance.

LE BRET: In truth,
  I could die contented were she to smile like that at me.

CADET 3: Yes, and have you noticed how
                    the whole camp smells of Morning Glory?

CADET 4: I think it's Lilac.

CADET 5:   Lavender!

CADET 6:   No, I believe that's Rose.

CYRANO: Gentlemen, it is Lily. Trust me; I have the -

CADET 7 *(interrupting Cyrano's "nose")*: If only
  it smelled of food instead!

LE BRET: For shame! Feast your eyes. Forget your belly.

ROXANE: It must be the looming fight.
                I, too, sir, have a soldier's appetite. Let's see:
  partridge pie *(- the Cadets moan quietly)*, fresh fruit,
  fine wine…*(More moaning.)* And for dessert – a sweet pastry!
    (Moans.) Would someone be so kind
                              as to bring that bill-of-fare to me?

(There is an embarrassed silence.)

CHRISTIAN: Roxane. We haven't –

ROXANE: checked my carriage? Its driver you may know.

(The Cadets storm the rampart.)

CYRANO: Cousin, could it possibly be - ?

SENTRY *(his head appearing, his mouth so stuffed he's almost unintelligible)*: It's Ragueneau!

CADETS *(to Christian, Le Bret and Cyrano)*:   Ragueneau!

(The pastry cook poet is helped over the rampart carrying a large basket. His feet never touch the ground.)

ROXANE: Poor boys.

CYRANO *(kissing her hand)*: Good angel.

(The Cadets stand Ragueneau on the basket.)

CADETS: Our hero!

LE BRET: Speech!

CADETS & CHRISTIAN: Bravo! Bravo!

RAGUENEAU: Thank Roxane
  for this fine feast. I only did the cooking –
                              she cooked-up the plan.
  Ho! The Spaniards, basking in her smile,
                              smiled upon my basket.
  If they questioned anything – well, they never thought to ask it.
    Wait! An homage *(looking at Roxane)*:

    "To Venus who the enemy did so admire
   that they paid no mind to this aged Vulcan
       (indicating himself) busy at his fire!"
  *(Cheers. Ragueneau gets down from the box and
  lifts its lid.)* I tell you, Christian,
       this wife of yours is wise as an old owl.
  While the Spaniards all adored the Fair,
       they overlooked the "Fowl!"

*(He holds up a cooked chicken. Gasps, applause.
Ragueneau and Roxane begin serving the "banquet." All
sit and eat ravenously. Soon the Sentry's head reappears.)*

SENTRY: Hey, no fair! The food is out of reach!

LE BRET *(carrying more food toward him)*: Keep guard!
  I'll – *(Noticing; to others)* Uh-oh, here comes de Guiche!
 (To Ragueneau) Close your basket! Hide!
      (To all) Everything out of sight!

*(In an instant, the feast has been hidden –
in tents, under hats and cloaks, etc. -
and the Cadets again prepare for battle. De
Guiche re-enters, stops, and sniffs the air.)*

DE GUICHE: What smells good?

LE BRET: Uh...Gunpowder! Men, pack it tight!

(The Cadets load their muskets, smiling.)

DE GUICHE *(suspicious)*: They look happy.

LE BRET: At the thought of battle!

DE GUICHE: Hmm.
 ...I've ordered a cannon brought here; that'll
 help some.

LE BRET: Thank you, sir!

DE GUICHE *(to Roxane)*: And so, what have you decided?

ROXANE: I stay.

DE GUICHE: ...Then so do I.

LE BRET: What?

DE GUICHE: I could not abide it
 an instant, leaving a woman behind while I was to...

CHRISTIAN: run?

DE GUICHE *(giving Christian one of his looks)*: Now,
 someone hand me a musket.

LE BRET *(shocked)*: What?

DE GUICHE: A musket. ...It's a gun.

CYRANO: Sir, you show courage.
 (To others) Here's a true Gascon! ...In spite of the lace.
 What say you, Cadets;
     shall we let our new brother stuff his face?

DE GUICHE: There's food?

RAGUENEAU *(appearing)*: A feast!

DE GUICHE: Ragueneau!

ROXANE: Come, Colonel de Guiche,
                        and join our heroes' banquet.
   It is well past-due.

DE GUICHE *(after a moment)*: Madame, no thank you.

ROXANE: Please, you need not stand on etiquette.

DE GUICHE *(with his old haughtiness)*: Nonsense,
  I simply refuse your scraps.
          (In a whisper)   Let these courageous men eat
   all.

CYRANO *(having overheard)*: Cadets,
       let us salute our Colonel. Everyone, on your feet!
   (The Cadets rise, raise their swords in sharp salute,
   and remain still, until the salute is returned. Cyrano
   then addresses de Guiche)   It's good to be hungry…

DE GUICHE: …for Spanish blood.
                    Yes, I will fight today as I am.

LE BRET: Sir, will you honor us with an inspection?

DE GUICHE *(to Roxane)*:   If you will take my arm, Madame?

(She does so. They accompany Le Bret offstage.)

CYRANO: Christian! *(Christian crosses to him; Ragueneau*
   attends to the others.)   Before you talk to Roxane,
                 just a word or two to the wise.
   If she should speak about your letters, you mustn't…

CHRISTIAN: Yes?

CYRANO: Well, show surprise.

CHRISTIAN: Surprise – why?

CYRANO: You may have written to her
                a bit more than you thought.

CHRISTIAN: Oh, have I?

CYRANO: Probably so.
        And now that Roxane is here you ought –

CHRISTIAN: - to know?

CYRANO: Yes.

CHRISTIAN: We've been blockaded here for a month!
                            How could you send - ?

CYRANO: Perfectly simple.
            Rising before daybreak, I managed to wend –

CHRISTIAN: Just how often did *I* write to her?
                        Two times a week?
    Three? Four?

CYRANO: A bit more.

CHRISTIAN: Every day?! Come, Cyrano, speak!

CYRANO: Yes, every day….twice.

CHRISTIAN *(angrily)*: Very nice!

                    You got so carried away you risked your life!
     If you ask me-

CYRANO *(seeing Roxane approaching)*: I don't!
     Now, hush.

ROXANE *(calling)*: Christian! Cyrano!

CYRANO: Not in front of your wife.

ROXANE *(returning)*: My two dearest Cadets,
                    from the Inspection I've "retreated." What a bore!
     Anyway, I could not endure being apart from you a minute more.

CHRISTIAN *(pulling her aside)*: Roxane,
     please do tell me what it is that brought you to this hell?

ROXANE: Your letters, of course.
                    So many; and each new one would excel
     the last in beauty and sincerity.

CHRISTIAN: You felt them to be...sincere?

ROXANE: How can you ask?
     Why, those letters are as true to me as they are dear!
     I have read them and again and yet ag-

CHRISTIAN: Doesn't it get...dull?

ROXANE: Not for a moment!
     Each page is like leaf fallen from your soul.
     And in your hand I hear that voice of what seems so long ago,
                    calling up to me in my balcony from the dark below.

CHRISTIAN: So you came?

ROXANE: Would Penelope have stayed home
                                    weaving at her loom
had Ulysses written from his war as does my devoted groom?

CHRISTIAN: But you –

ROXANE: Christian, I came here to ask of you your forgiveness,
and what better time to do so then when in death's near caress?
Forgive me, my dear, for the shallowness that I have shown
       in loving you, at first, for your beauty – and that alone.

CHRISTIAN: Oh, Roxane!

ROXANE: Oh, great soul!
             How you must have suffered from my false start –
to be early-on embraced for your form and face, yet not the part
       far more beautiful within.
                   Please know the shell of you I once did prize,
I no longer see at all –
                   now that I've come to look with clearer eyes.
             Your heart revealed in words,
                         it is now your *inner* self that I adore!

CHRISTIAN: Roxane, tell me – Were I less handsome…?

ROXANE: Then I should only love you more.

CHRISTIAN: Alas, I liked it best before. …And if…ugly?

ROXANE: I would love you still,
       and with all my being!

CHRISTIAN: Oh, God! *(Aside)* I think I am going to be ill.

ROXANE: My beloved, what is it? Have I somehow –

CHRISTIAN: No! …I just need a moment if you'll allow
   it, to have two words with -

ROXANE: But –

CHRISTIAN: Roxane, our happiness does deny
   the pleasure of your company
                    to my comrades who soon may die.
      I beseech you, go and smile at them for me.
   It may well be the last woman's smile they see.

ROXANE *(touched)*: Dear Christian.

CHRISTIAN: Go.
                Please. *(She does.)* Cyrano!

(Cyrano enters from his tent, armed for battle.)

CYRANO: What's wrong?

CHRISTIAN: She does not love me any more.

CYRANO: Christian, you are mistaken, I am sure.

CHRISTIAN: Roxane only loves my soul, and that means *you*!

CYRANO: No!

CHRISTIAN: Yes! And another thing – You love her, too.

CYRANO: That's nonsense!
         Hunger, my friend, has plainly addled your mind.

CHRISTIAN: My belly is empty, not my head.
                    Nor are my eyes blind

to what *"lies"* before them.
    (Cyrano begins to reply, but is interrupted.)
                        You once told me I was no fool.
I implore you; don't treat me as one now. It would be cruel.

CYRANO: Can you honestly believe for a moment
                      that I might love your wife?

CHRISTIAN: I know so, Cyrano.

CYRANO *(after a pause)*: …Well, yes, it's true.
                  But, Christian, upon my life -

CHRISTIAN: Then you must tell her.

CYRANO: I cannot. No!

CHRISTIAN: Why not?

CYRANO: Why, look! This *(- his nose)* thwarts Cupid's bow.

CHRISTIAN: She would love me still if I were ugly.

CYRANO: Roxane said that?

CHRISTIAN: Yes.

CYRANO: Really?

CHRISTIAN: So help me!

CYRANO: Well, that's good of her, but far too absurd.
            Christian, I shouldn't take her at her word.

CHRISTIAN: You talk to her.

CYRANO: Me?

CHRISTIAN: What have you to lose?
    Tell her everything! And let her choose
        between us.

CYRANO: No, Christian, I refuse
    to torture myself!

CHRISTIAN: A poor excuse.
    (Cynically) So your future happiness I should just go steal
            by simple virtue of my form's accursed appeal?

CYRANO: Tell me, is it better then that I destroy your happiness
    just because I'm able to say what you feel, but can't express?

CHRISTIAN: Cyrano, tell her – or I'll go out of my skull!
            Please. I am tired of being my own rival.

CYRANO: Christian –

CHRISTIAN: I will be loved for who I am, or not at all!
    Now, talk to her, no more to me. I'll go …check the firewall,
        and return to learn which of us she does prefer.

CYRANO: It will be you.

CHRISTIAN: God – I hope so, but will defer
    my rejoicing until I know. *(Calling)* Roxane!

CYRANO: No!

ROXANE *(coming, as do,
                separately, Le Bret and de Guiche)*: Yes, dear?

CHRISTIAN: Cyrano has something important for you to hear.

(She turns to Cyrano. Christian exits over the
rampart, following Le Bret and de Guiche who
continue their inspection.)

ROXANE: Important?

CYRANO *(distracted)*: He's gone...

ROXANE: Cousin?

CYRANO: Oh, it's nothing really, Roxane;
   only Christian would like me to ascertain...as best I can –

ROXANE: whether what I told him just now was true –

CYRANO: beyond doubt.
   ...Well, was it?

ROXANE: Yes! I said...

CYRANO *(smiling softly)*:   Go on; you need not hold-out.

ROXANE: I said only that I should love him even if he were...

CYRANO: Ugly?
   See, I don't mind.

ROXANE: Ugly, yes. *(A shot is heard offstage, followed*
   by several others. Ragueneau and the Cadets cross to the
   rampart.) Was that gunfire?

CYRANO *(dismissing this;*
                    compelling her attention): It would seem to be.

But, Roxane,
          surely you could not love him if he were…hideous?

ROXANE: Yes, even if hideous.

CYRANO: Oh, but surely not ridiculous?

ROXANE: Don't you see, he could never be ridiculous to me.

CYRANO: And you would love him so, as much as –

ROXANE: More! Infinitely!

CYRANO *(aside, excitedly,*
  as Roxane turns to the rampart): My God. It's true.
  A chance yet to be happy. *(To Roxane, drawing her back)*
                              …Roxane….listen…

LE BRET *(having quickly entered over the rampart,*
  calling in a low tone): Cyrano. *(Cyrano waves him off.*
  Then more adamantly) Cyrano, listen!

CYRANO: What?! *(Le Bret whispers in his ear.)* Ah.

ROXANE: What is it?

CYRANO *(stunned, to himself)*:   Gone.

LE BRET: Amen.

CYRANO *(still to self)*: All gone. I can never tell her now.

ROXANE *(to Le Bret)*:   Has something happened?

  (More gun shots are exchanged.)

LE BRET: Just that...the battle has begun.

ROXANE *(to Cyrano)*:   Then quickly, my dear friend,
   finish what you were saying before you have to go.

CYRANO: ...Just this, Roxane;
                       it is most important that you know
   that the spirit of dear Christian – that is, his soul was greater –

ROXANE: *"Was"*? Oh, no. *(De Guiche, Ragueneau,
   and several Cadets carry a limp Christian, stretched
   out on his cloak, back over the rampart. Roxane sees
   them.)* Christian!

LE BRET *(to Cyrano)*: On the first volley.

   *(Christian is put down on the ground. Roxane
   kneels beside him, desperate to save him.)*

DE GUICHE *(to Cyrano)*:   Try to placate her
   until I can arrange for her safe transport.

   (Exits.)

LE BRET *(to Cadets)*: Cadets!

   *(Le Bret and the Cadets follow de Guiche over the rampart.
   Roxane dips a strip of linen torn from her dress in a helmet
   full of water brought over by Ragueneau.)*

CYRANO *(low and quick in Christian's ear
                while Roxane is busy with the above)*: I have told
   her. She loves *you.*

CHRISTIAN *(faintly)*: Rox...

ROXANE *(holding him)*: My darling.

Oh, Cyrano his cheek grows cold
against mine!

CHRISTIAN *(struggling to finish, barely audible)*: Roxane,
you must... promise me...

*(Unable to speak another word,
he gestures weakly towards Cyrano.)*

ROXANE: Anything, my beloved – eternally!

*(His hand drops, inadvertently on the letter
protruding from his shirt.)*

CYRANO: Roxane, I –

ROXANE *(to Christian)*: What's this, a letter?
(Showing it to Cyrano) Over his heart.
*(She gives it to her cousin to unfold for her.
He does so and hands it back to her.)* For me?

CYRANO: One more testament of his love and art.

(Christian dies.)

ROXANE: Christian - ? Christian! *(Quietly)* Oh, no.

*(An explosion lands just over the rampart.
Shouts and cries are heard.)*

CYRANO: Roxane, I have to go.
My other comrades –

ROXANE: Wait. Just a little. Please. ....Christian is dead,

and no one here knew him as you did. …I see that you, too, shed
tears for this finest of men. How we both shall miss him.

CYRANO: Beyond words, Roxane.

I would sooner have lost a limb.

ROXANE: He was a hero, wasn't he?

CYRANO: Yes, Roxane. Undeniably.

ROXANE: Of profound mind.

CYRANO: Yes, Roxane.

ROXANE: A spirit that shined.

CYRANO: Yes.

ROXANE: And a heart too large for commonplace mankind.

CYRANO: Oh, yes, Roxane!

*(A distant trumpet sounds amidst the noise
of battle. Ragueneau climbs the rampart.)*

RAGUENEAU: A trumpet! Can
   it be?

DE GUICHE *(wounded, coming over the
   rampart)*: The army is returning! She can make safe passage,
   if only *we* can hold on.

CYRANO: We'll die trying; you have my pledge!

ROXANE: On the letter – His blood.
                          ...Oh, and also the mark of a tear.

(She faints into Cyrano's arms. A loud report.
The helmet that Ragueneau is still holding on
the rampart is shot right out of his hands.)

RAGUENEAU: Our goose, I fear, is cooked!

CYRANO: Ragueneau, help get her out of here!
  Follow the Colonel.
              (To de Guiche) Sir, you have proved yourself today.
  Now you must take care of her.

DE GUICHE *(taking Roxane in his arms)*: As you wish.
                          (To Ragueneau) Come, this way!
  (Again to Cyrano) Hold on just a bit longer
                          and God may yet spare us.

CYRANO: We're the Cadets of Gascony.

DE GUICHE & CYRANO: See you in Paris!

(A huge explosion. The Sentry flies over the rampart, dead.)

CYRANO: Go!

(De Guiche and Ragueneau exit one side of the stage as a
wounded Le Bret makes his way over back into camp over
the rampart, along with Cadets 3, 4, 5, and 6. Even while
climbing over the rampart, they still fight off several Span-
iards, before collapsing on the ground.)

LE BRET: We are breaking! I am twice wounded.

CYRANO: Hold on, friend. Do not quit the campaign.
  This day will be ours, I swear!

        For, you see, I have two deaths to avenge of Spain –

LE BRET: Two?

CYRANO: Christian's…and that of my own happiness.
                      (Shouting) Music, Cadet!
 (Cadet 5 begins playing the Gascon theme on the fife as
 Cyrano draws his sword and lifts one of the pieces of
 drapery as a huge banner.) Let us give those Spaniards
                  a welcome they'll not live to forget!
  Forward, my brave Gascons!

            Soon on every enemy's last breath
  will be the question:

      "Who are these few who are so fond of death?"
  And we respond,
  our fury donned:
 (Waving the banner and singing amidst the cacophony of
 battle)   We are the Cadets of Gascony –
             The defenders of liberty.
         (Cadet 6 joins in on the drum.)
      We send to their final resting-place
 (He rushes to the rampart followed by the others who now
 add their voices to the song.)
        All of those fool enough to face –

(The rest of the words are drowned-out by the deafening din
of war. Lights out, except for the flashes that accompanying
explosions. Cadets and Spaniards fall. The rousing Gascon
theme continues vocally and/or instrumentally, and as the
scene-change completes, the music cross-fades into a period
hymn, the Cadets' voices replaced by that of a choir of nuns.)

Scene iii: Cyrano's Gazette

*(Lights up on the park of the Convent of the Ladies of the
Cross in Paris, fifteen years later, 1655. It is late October
and leaves are falling – large leaves. A tree – or simply its
red canopy – is center. French words are scrawled on its fo-
liage, each leaf suggesting a torn piece of a letter. Beneath
the tree sits an embroidery frame and beside it a simple
chair. An unfinished tapestry is on the frame and baskets with
skeins of yarn beneath. Two nuns converge on Mother Marguerite, as the distant singing of unseen Sisters continues as
underscoring – Convent choir practice.)*

SISTER CLAIRE: Mother,
          Sister Marthe stole a plum from the pie this morning.

MOTHER MARGUERITE: Sister Marthe,
              this will be your last warning, your last warning!

SISTER MARTHE: Well,
   Sister Claire looked in the glass again. I couldn't stop her.

MOTHER MARGUERITE: Sister Claire,
              you know that is most improper, most improper!

SISTER CLAIRE: But Mother, it was the briefest of looks!

SISTER MARTHE: The smallest of plums!

MOTHER MARGUERITE *(with mock severity)*: Still,
          I shall have to tell Monsieur de Bergerac when he comes.

SISTER CLAIRE: Please don't! He shall think us garish

SISTER MARTHE: and greedy.

MOTHER MARGUERITE *(taking their hands,*
                                    laughing): And good!

SISTER CLAIRE: This is Saturday; he should be here soon.

MOTHER MARGUERITE: In all likelihood.

SISTER MARTHE: Likelihood?
  He hasn't missed his weekly visit in some ten years.

SISTER CLAIRE: Twelve!

MOTHER MARGUERITE: Fourteen.
  Ever since his cousin came to live with us, my dears.

SISTER MARTHE: Think of it!
                    To be so constant for such a great while.

MOTHER MARGUERITE: And may God bless him,
                    for no one else can bring a smile
  to Madame Madeleine's grave countenance,
    I dare say, no one else in all of France!

SISTER CLAIRE: Monsieur makes *all* of us laugh
                    with his gentle teases.
        I've made him an angel cake. I do hope it pleases
  him.

SISTER MARTHE: Regrettably it can not,
                    whereas my homemade Sorbet de Banane -

MOTHER MARGUERITE: Sister.

SISTER CLAIRE: Oh, I've tasted that.
                    All it's fit to fill is the "garbage *de* can."

MOTHER MARGUERITE: Sister!

SISTER MARTHE: Well, your cake is far too rich;
                                it will only make our dear guest sick!

MOTHER MARGUERITE *(silencing them)*: Perhaps he'd
    best be served...by prayer.

SISTER MARTHE: Oh, but he's not a good Catholic!

SISTER CLAIRE: Yes, but some day we shall convert him.

MOTHER MARGUERITE: No, you shall let him be, let him be!
    I am afraid that if you torment Monsieur,

                                he may come less frequently.

SISTER MARTHE: But Mother Marguerite –

SISTER CLAIRE: - what of God?

MOTHER MARGUERITE: Oh, I'm quite certain God's well-
    acquainted with our friend.

SISTER MARTHE: But each visit, he makes sure to tell
    me, to my deep dismay: "Sister, I ate meat Friday!"

SISTER CLAIRE: He says the very same to me!

MOTHER MARGUERITE: In truth, on his last visit
                he hadn't eaten *any*thing for two days, maybe three.

SISTER MARTHE: Who told you so?

MOTHER MARGUERITE: His friend, Monsieur Le Bret.
    It seems that our favorite guest is, alas, quite poor, quite poor.

SISTER CLAIRE: Is there no merciful soul
   to offer him succor?

MOTHER MARGUERITE: He is very proud;
                                    any help he would deplore.
(Roxane appears, dressed in black with a widow's veil.
De Guiche, magnificently grown old, walks beside her.)
        Now off to choir! Madame Madeleine has another visitor.

SISTER MARTHE *(to Sister Claire)*: It's the Marshall,
   is it not?

SISTER CLAIRE *(looking toward de Guiche)*:   I think so.
                                It's been months since he's seen her.

MOTHER MARGUERITE: He is a busy man. There is the
   Court, the Camp – a world of care. Now, shoo, shoo! Shoo!

*(They all exit. De Guiche and Roxane approach the
embroidery frame.)*

DE GUICHE: And so you remain here, forever in mourning?

ROXANE: Yes; well at peace in this milieu.

DE GUICHE: And still faithful?

ROXANE: As ever.

DE GUICHE *(with some uneasiness)*: Am I perhaps forgiven?

ROXANE: Need you ask, sir?
                You have been since I have come to live in
   this quiet convent all those many years ago.
And, too, there is much that is forgotten.

DE GUICHE: Although
   you still wear Christian's last letter near your heart, I see.

ROXANE *(touching a chain around her neck)*: Yes,
               it hangs here, much like a holy reliquary.

DE GUICHE: So long dead, and yet you love him still.

ROXANE: He lives inside of me, if you will.

DE GUICHE: Yes, there are some memories one must not let go.
   (After a brief silence) And tell me,
                 do you still see much of Cyrano?

ROXANE: Every week!
      My old friend takes the place of my Gazette,
  bringing me the news each Saturday. The Sisters set
   a chair for him just where you're standing, beneath this tree.
         I sit and wait for him, doing my embroidery.
        The hour strikes, and on its very last stroke, I hear -
  like clockwork - the tap of a cane. And who should appear?

DE GUICHE: I can't guess.

ROXANE: My dear cousin Cyrano with a nasty smirk
   on his face.

DE GUICHE: A smirk?

ROXANE: He scoffs at my eternal needlework.
   Then tells the story of the week, and so the evening passes.

   (Le Bret appears.)

ROXANE: But look, Le Bret!

DE GUICHE *(quietly)*: It seems in one of his usual morasses.

ROXANE *(as Le Bret reaches them)*: How
 goes it with our friend?

LE BRET: Oh, not well at all, Madame!

ROXANE: He exaggerates!

LE BRET: No, it's as I've said. And I am
    sorry to see such loneliness and misery.
 I predicted this, but would he listen to me?
   And I tell you both, he continues to make new enemies
    with those satires he writes attacking gross hypocrisies.

DE GUICHE: Attacking *all*!

ROXANE: Yet none would challenge him;
                                his sword still strikes fear.

DE GUICHE *(shrugging)*: Who knows?

LE BRET: It's not violence that worries me, but rather the sheer
    weight of his solitude and poverty – an Autumn
       of the spirit – that I start to see fall upon him.

DE GUICHE: No need to pity him too much.

LE BRET: My Lord Marshall, sir?

DE GUICHE: Cyrano still lives the life he always did prefer
    to lead. In thought, word, and act he continues to be free.
      He has nothing; I everything… and that includes Envy.
    (After a reflective moment) Suffice it to say, sir,
                          I should be proud to shake his hand.

ROXANE: The sentiment does you honor.

LE BRET: That, none would countermand!

DE GUICHE: Now I must go. Adieu.

LE BRET *(bowing)*: Sir.

ROXANE: And I shall walk you to the gate.

(They start off as the choir practice comes to an end.)

DE GUICHE *(suddenly)*: Monsieur Le Bret, one moment.
                    (To Roxane) Pardon me; and kindly do wait.
   (In a low tone to Le Bret) It is true that no one dares
                                openly attack you friend,
yet there are more subtle means by which he might meet his end.

LE BRET: You've heard something?

DE GUICHE *(nodding)*: At court, uttered confidentially,
        that Cyrano might somehow die – "accidentally."
    Tell him to be careful.

LE BRET: Careful?! He is coming here.
    I'll warn him, of course, but you know he will only jeer
    at the –

(Two nuns enter, each carrying a musical instrument.)

ROXANE: Hello, dear Sisters. Tell me, is choir done so soon?

SISTER 3: Monsieur Ragueneau has asked to see you.

SISTER 4: He seems all aswoon!

ROXANE: Bring him here, please.
  (They exit. To the men) He comes I suspect for sympathy.

LE BRET: Ah, Madame; you are right about that, I guarantee
  it!

ROXANE: The poor dear fellow.

DE GUICHE: Not more marriage trouble?

LE BRET: To say the least.
  He went to the abbey about it –

ROXANE: and Lise ran off with the priest.

RAGUENEAU *(entering hurriedly, followed by the two nuns)*:
  Ah, Madame!

ROXANE: Friend, first tell all to Le Bret. I'll be right back.

  *(She exits with de Guiche; the two nuns
  occupy themselves upstage.)*

RAGUENEAU: I'm glad you're here.
  She need not know so soon.

LE BRET: De Bergerac?

RAGUENEAU: I went to visit his room today,
                    and saw him come out the door.
  So I hurried to catch-up, little suspecting what was in store
  for our friend. At a window overhead...a working man...

LE BRET: Go on!

RAGUENEAU *(overcome)*: Oh, was it by chance,
                        or might it have been some plan?

LE BRET: Ragueneau!

RAGUENEAU: A lone working man…
                with a great log of wood…

LE BRET: Oh no.

RAGUENEAU: …let it fall.

LE BRET: Cyrano?

RAGUENEAU: Who else could have withstood
  such a terrible blow to the head?

LE BRET: Then he is not dead?

RAGUENEAU: Just barely alive.
    I carried him home and into his bed.
  Le Bret, have you seen his room?

LE BRET *(dismissing the question)*:   Is he in pain?

RAGUENEAU: Unconscious.

LE BRET: A doctor?

RAGUENEAU: One came – for charity. I put up such a fuss.

LE BRET: Poor Cyrano! We must not tell Roxane all at once.
  What did the doctor say?

RAGUENEAU: Just lots of mumbles and grunts!

Something about fever and lesions – I hardly know!
Oh, if you'd seen him, his skull wrapped in bandages so...
But he is home all-alone now with no one nearby,
and I'm convinced should he try to get up, he will die!

LE BRET: Then we must go to him, Ragueneau, without delay!
          (Ragueneau starts off the way he came.)
      No, follow me! Through the Chapel; it's the shortest way.

RAGUENEAU *(looking to where Le Bret has pointed him)*:
                    We'll have to push through quite a crowd.

LE BRET *(to Ragueneau as he draws his sword and
          heads off)*: Anyone blocks my path, gets ploughed!

      (Roxane re-enters to see them disappearing.)

ROXANE *(calling)*: Monsieurs! *(The men continue off. To
      herself)* Well, Ragueneau must have been exceedingly tragic.
      *(She sits at her embroidery frame and watches the leaves
      fall for a moment.)* Autumn: such melancholy beauty.
                                It has a strange magic
      all its own. *(She begins her work as Sisters Claire and
      Marthe carry a great chair, each vying to be the one to
      set it just so under the tree.)* Ah, the old chair
          for my old friend.

BOTH SISTERS: Our best one!

      *(They give each other a nasty look. The
      bell clock begins to chime, seven times.)*

ROXANE: The hour strikes!

SISTER CLAIRE: He will be here before its chime is done.

SISTER MARTHE *(one upping her)*: As always.

ROXANE: Thank you, Sisters. *(They scurry off.*
  The clock finishes striking the hour. No Cyrano.)
                    Odd. He's never been late before.
  Perhaps Mother Marguerite
              has barred him from the convent door
        until he at last agrees to repent for every sin
  of his. If so, he shall never make it in!
        (A slow tapping is heard.) Ah, my cousin!
  *(Back to work. Cyrano appears, very pale, his hat drawn over
  his eyes. He walks slowly, nodding to the two nuns he passes
  as they linger upstage with their instruments. It is clearly an
  effort for him to stay upright, and he leans heavily on his
  cane.Without looking up from her embroidering, Roxane greets
  Cyrano playfully.)* Late for the first time in fourteen years.

CYRANO *(reaching the chair, collapsing into it)*: Yes,
                              I'm rather vexed.
          I was detained by a visitor I did not expect.

ROXANE: How troublesome.

CYRANO: Inopportune.

ROXANE: Someone you know?

CYRANO: In a sense.
  Or perhaps better instead I should say: an old acquaintance.

ROXANE: Well, my dear cousin,
  I do hope that you told him to go away.

CYRANO: For the time being.
  …I said: "Excuse me, but this is Saturday!

I have a prior engagement, one that I will not miss,
 even for you. Come back in an hour."

ROXANE: Now, you hear this;
 one brief hour hardly will suffice.
                        Your friend will simply have to wait
 'til well past dark.

 (A few leaves fall. Cyrano watches their descent.)

CYRANO *(gently)*: I think I may have to leave you
                              before it gets that late.

ROXANE: I shan't let you.

CYRANO *(teasing)*: Nor ever let me see
                    the end of these embroideries!

ROXANE: There are several nuns in the park
                if you are looking for someone to tease.

CYRANO *(calling)*: Sisters!
    If you would be so kind, please play something…autumnal.

ROXANE: No taunts? You seem rather subdued today.

CYRANO *(as several more leaves fall)*:   No, just made humble
 by the grace of falling leaves.
                (Music begins.) They do know how to let go,
 don't they? So brief a fall from branch to earth,
                                    and yet they show
            us one last great flutter of…panache, in their dying.
  Dropping with such spirit – It is a fall that seems like flying.

ROXANE: You are sad.

CYRANO: No.

ROXANE: Then let the leaves fall as they may,
                         and you be my Gazette.

CYRANO: Ah! Yes, of course, my dear Roxane,
                         how ever could I forget?
  Saturday – the last: he King became ill
            guzzling wine of a none-too-vintage season.
  Hence, the vineyard was brought forthwith
      before the Court and executed for High-Treason.

ROXANE *(laughing)*: And what of His Majesty?

CYRANO: With the vineyard skived,
                         Louis miraculously revived.
  On Sunday a Bishop was sent to heaven,
            though I've heard no reports that he arrived.

ROXANE: Monsieur de Bergerac!
  Your tongue is most wicked.

CYRANO: True; I haven't a "*lick*" of shame.

ROXANE: Now, I'll hear no more of Sunday.

CYRANO: Then on to dreary Monday,
                         which was much the same
  as every other Monday – as quiet as this park.

ROXANE: Do tell. Why so?

CYRANO: Oh, well you know…

ROXANE & CYRANO: All the theatres are dark.

CYRANO: But, now, Tuesday was aglow!
At the Queen's ball, they lit well over seven hundred tapers.

ROXANE: How lush!

CYRANO: I haven't an exact count;
                    alas, the ensuing fire burnt-down the newspapers.

ROXANE: Oh, hush!

CYRANO: On Wednesday,
 the actor Montfleury's irksome little poodle was finally "fixed."
   I suggested the same procedure for its master –
                              an idea disappointingly nixed.

ROXANE: Cousin! This is conversation hardly fitting for
 a convent.

CYRANO: You might say it's "un*convent*ional."

ROXANE: I'd rather say "Move on!"

CYRANO: So I intuit.
 Well, then Thursday:
   Marshall de Guiche gave a major speech at the Academy.

ROXANE: Did it go well?

CYRANO: Oh, yes. I was able to sleep quite soundly through it.
 Friday, Ragueneau lit his ovens for the last,
                and now instead he lights the lights for Moliere.
   And Saturday – today…

 (His eyes close; his head sinks back.)

ROXANE: Cyrano! *(She rushes to him.)*

CYRANO *(opening his eyes; vaguely)*: What?

ROXANE: You fainted!

*(He sees Roxane bending over him and pulls his hat
further down over his head, leaning away from her.)*

CYRANO: It's nothing. Sorry to give you a scare.

ROXANE: But what is it? What's wrong?

CYRANO: Oh…now and then….
                    you know…that old wound I got at Arras.

ROXANE *(moving to comfort him)*: My poor friend.

CYRANO: No! Really. …Please, Roxane; sit.
              It will soon not matter. This all shall pass.
    (Forcing a smile) There!   ….Near gone.

ROXANE *(still standing)*: It seems that we all carry
              old wounds never quite healed. I have mine right here
    at my breast. The writing has all but faded away.
                          Not so the stain of blood and tear.

CYRANO: His letter!
              …Did you not say I might read it one day?

ROXANE: You wish to?

CYRANO: I do now, yes. *(Roxane gives him the
    little silken bag from around her neck.)* May I open it?

ROXANE: You may,
    indeed.

(She goes back to her embroidery. Cyrano
unfolds the letter. Twilight begins to fall ever so gradually.)

CYRANO *(reading)*: "Roxane, farewell, for today I die."

ROXANE *(surprised)*:   Aloud?

CYRANO: "I think it will be this evening, and my heart is bowed
    by the weight of the love I bear for you, yet can not impart,
      and nor now ever shall. Yet heavier still upon my heart,
    Roxane, is this – that never more shall my eyes kiss the sight
      of your every splendid grace, - "

ROXANE: How you read it!

CYRANO: " – and delight
    in even the slightest of your gestures.
    (Unnoticed by Roxane who is busy working, his arm falls
    to his side, the letter still held in his hand. His eyes close.
          He is reciting it now by heart.) When I recall
    how you'd brush from your eyes
          that lock of hair that'd always fall,
  my heart cries out - "

ROXANE *(stopping her needlework)*: Christian's letter
          …and yet you read it so –

CYRANO: "cries out to you: Farewell, my dearest, - "

ROXANE: In a voice I know –

CYRANO: "my treasure, my heart!…"

ROXANE: that I heard spoken long ago, beneath –

CYRANO: "My own angel, know this: *(As he continues,*
Roxane slowly, quietly crosses behind his chair, unobserved,
and sees that he is not reading, but reciting the letter from
         his own memory.) All that I have that I can bequeath
         to you is a vow of eternal love. I am never
away from you. Even today, as I journey…wherever,
    I shall remain the one who loves you – beyond all measure,
    beyond – "

ROXANE: For fourteen years,
                      through all our Saturdays of leisure,
  you played your part oh so convincingly -
    the droll friend steadfastly amusing me.

CYRANO: Roxane!

ROXANE: And it was you, Cyrano; you all along!

CYRANO: No!

ROXANE: Each time you spoke my name
  I should have known.

CYRANO: You're wrong!
  It was not I.

ROXANE: Oh, but it was.

CYRANO: I swear –

ROXANE: That generous lie!
  The letters – That was you.

CYRANO: No!

ROXANE: The voice in the dark.

CYRANO: Upon my
  word of honor, I say "No!"

ROXANE: And...the Soul! ...It was all you.

CYRANO: No, Christian.
  It was he who loved you; not I.

ROXANE: You. And still. As no one has...or can.

CYRANO (his voice much weaker): No.

ROXANE: Your voice, this time, betrays you.

CYRANO: No, my love, I love you not.

ROXANE (after a silence): So much I thought
                    forever lost to me, and now this caveat!
  Oh, but why stay so long unspoken?
                    You should have known far better
  how much you gave me, not poor Christian.
                         Why, even on this letter
  worn so close to my heart, the tear is yours.

CYRANO: Yes, but the blood is his.

ROXANE: Then why break the silence now?

CYRANO: Why? Because –

  (Le Bret and Ragueneau enter on the run.)

LE BRET: I knew it! Here he is!

RAGUENEAU: Such folly!

LE BRET *(to the musician nuns)*: Quickly, find a doctor!

RAGUENEAU *(quietly)*: And a priest.

*(The two nuns exit, their underscoring having stopped
at Le Bret and Ragueneau's noisy entrance.)*

CYRANO *(smiling, trying unsuccessfully to rise)*: Ah,
                                        so I am found.

RAGUENEAU *(to Roxane)*: He's done it now all right,
    coming here!

LE BRET *(to Cyrano)*: Damn well put yourself in the ground!

ROXANE: He – oh, God…the faintness…that was –

CYRANO: Nothing!   …But I did not complete
    my Gazette. Saturday – today: One hour before he was to meet
        his dear cousin, Monsieur de Bergerac was…assassinated.

*(He removes his hat, revealing his bloody
bandaged head.)*

ROXANE: Dearest Cyrano, what have they done to you?!

CYRANO: Only frustrated
    my intent of dying a hero – sword in hand.
                        How Fate loves a jest!
    Who'd have guessed –
    a cowardly ambush is what has laid me to my rest.

A gutter for my last battlefield, a lackey my noble foe,
a log of wood his weapon! It seems only all too apropos.
  Finally, I have missed everything –

                              even a death of my own choosing.
  (Ragueneau breaks down.)
    Stop that, friend. *(He takes Ragueneau's hand.)*
      Should you write my story, do make it suitably amusing.

RAGUENEAU: I'm not a poet any more.

CYRANO: You will always be a poet;
  though – yes, I know –
    you now have work with Monsieur Moliere.

RAGUENEAU: No, it
    is over with as of tomorrow! Today they played "Scapin,"
    and I was shocked to find that he had stolen an entire scene
                      from you – word for word!

LE BRET *(furious)*: Stole a scene?! My sword!

CYRANO: Bah! At least the thief showed good taste.
  (To Ragueneau) The scene went well?

RAGUENEAU: Ah, how they laughed!

CYRANO: Good. Then it did not go to waste.
  …And, after all,
          has not the whole of my life been faithfully like this?

    I, a voice in the shadows,
                  while another wins the applause – or kiss.

ROXANE: Oh, where is that doctor?!

(She moves to exit.)

CYRANO *(grabbing her hand)*: There's no need, Roxane.
                              And please don't go away,
for, you see, I may no longer be here when you return.

ROXANE *(lifting her veil)*:   No, don't say
    such things! You must live! I love you! Live!

CYRANO: Were this but a fairy tale!
    When Beauty said "I love you" to the Beast, then –
                              well, just like your veil -
    his ugliness was lifted. Alas, that is not my story-line,
    as you can plainly see.

(The moon rises.)

ROXANE: I have done this to you! The fault is mine!

CYRANO: You, Roxane? Why, no.
                    On the contrary! I have never known
    a woman's kindness, sympathy, and care equal to your own.
    You have given me friendship all my life –
                              through this ignoble end.

LE BRET *(pointing to the moon)*: Cyrano,
        you are being looked upon by another old friend.

CYRANO *(smiling)*: I see.

ROXANE: I have loved but one man in my life,
                              and I have lost him twice.

CYRANO *(still looking at the moon)*: And so, Le Bret,

without having to invent any flying device,
I make my way after all towards that divine celestial light.

LE BRET: No! Too idiotic, too unjust!
                    It simply is not fair or right
for such a spirit, such a great heart, to die this way!

CYRANO: Ah, but it would seem Destiny disagrees.

LE BRET: Damn! -

CYRANO: And here you are - growling again!
    Perhaps it is time, old friend, to leave the "bark" to the trees.
    (Then half-rising, his eyes turning upward) And now,
    you must forgive me for I can no longer delay.
    Look there, do you see?
        This moonbeam has come to lead me away.
    *(He falls back into his chair, half-fainting. The sobbing
      of Roxane draws him back to reality. He gently lowers
      her veil back over her face.)*   My dearest,
                I would not want you to mourn for Christian any less.
    He was a loving, good and noble man. But might I only press
        upon you to give a double meaning to your widow's veil,
            and mourning him, mourn me a little, too…

ROXANE *(weeping)*:   My love, without fail!
    Oh, you know I will!

    *(Cyrano shivers violently, as if trying to shake
      something off of him.)*

CYRANO: No! Not here! Not thus! Not sitting in a chair!
    *(He suddenly stands, and stares straight ahead. The
      others spring forward to help him. But he motions them*

away.) I'll have no help – no help from anyone!
 (To his newest enemy) Ah, Monsieur – C'est la guerre.

*(He draws his cane, as though a sword, still
staring at someone nobody else can see.)*

ROXANE: Cyrano!

LE BRET *(breaking down)*: My most cherished friend.

RAGUENEAU *(quietly)*:   Delirious. I fear the end
 is nigh.

CYRANO: Ah, you snoutless skullhead,
 I see that you are staring at my nose.
 Face it, I am at the advantage if, over it,
 we should come to *blows.*
 Eh? What's that? "Hopeless," you say, "futile to resist?"
 Oh, that's quite plain.
But even better than fighting to win is the chance to fight in vain!
 So! A hundred against one.
 And who are all your new recruits? Of course;
I recognize them now –
 old enemies of mine; a most imposing force.
 (He lunges at the air.) Falsehood?!
 There *(thrusting)* There! And *Compromise!*
 (A feint and thrust) Ha! Got you, right between the eyes!
Now comes, *Prejudice!* Take that *(a hit)* and This
 *(- a fatal one! Then quickly parrying an imagined
 blow from behind)* What!? *Cowardice*;
I should have guessed. *(A riposte.)*
 Surrender? Never! *(He ducks...)* Ah ha, you miss!
(...and lunges, finishing off that opponent, too).
 But who is this? Draw closer!
 ...A nose-length's away... Ah, *Vanity!*

I knew in the end that it would be you who'd get the best of me.
(Swinging his cane wildly now) But I fight on! I figh-
(He stops, gasping for breath. When he speaks
again, his tone is much changed.)
Yes, all of my laurels you have riven,
and my roses, too. However, there is one thing I've not given
up to you. As I now enter before God – with a grand salute
sweeping all the stars from heaven's gate (- spoken
as he sweeps his cane high over his head)
– my most precious attribute
I'll still possess,
locked forever in my Soul's own deepest cache,
unscathed even by death. ...And that is...

(The cane drops from his hand. He staggers and
falls into his moonbeam and the arms of Le Bret
and Ragueneau.)

ROXANE (leaning over him and kissing his brow): And
that is...?

CYRANO (opening his eyes and smiling at her):   My panache.

(Music. His eyes close as an oversized red leaf
flutters slowly to the ground in the light of Cyrano's
moonbeam. Curtain.)

The End

A Word on the Design

As the play's poetry is intended to convey a stage world both romantic and idealized—outside the realm of everyday reality—a highly stylized design will serve the same end. At least one major set piece or prop in every scene should be preposterously large, a visual reiteration of Cyrano's perception of his nose. Also encouraged is the incorporation of words wherever they can be placed. Even the preferably raked stage floor itself can become a canvas for Cyrano's last missive to Roxane—preferably in its original French.* Throughout the script, stage directions refer to other such possibilities.

Similarly, aspects of costuming can help inform the world of the play. Deliberately exaggerated period styles and cuts, and even the appliqué of French words on various articles of the characters' clothing are options to consider.

As for sound design, underscoring is called for throughout the play, sometimes provided by characters playing period instruments. There are also several songs. Two are sung by the Cadets, and another, a remembered childhood melody, by Cyrano and Roxane. Whereas these certainly can be created anew for each production, there is a lovely score created for the original staging by composer Ron Barnett. Interested parties can reach Mr. Barnett via e-mail at: Chreode@juno.com or c/o Fulton Opera House, P.O. Box 1865 Lancaster PA 17608.

> *Roxane, adieu, je vais mourir!
> C'est pour ce soir, je crois, ma bien-aimée!
> J'ai l'ame lourde encor d'amour inexprimée,
> Et je meurs! jamais plus, jamais mes yeux grisés,
> Mes regards dont c'était les frémissantes fetes:
> J'en revois un petit qui vous est familier
> Ne baiseront au vol les gestes que vous faites:
> Pour toucher votre front, et je voudrais crier.
> Et je crie: Adieu! Ma chère, ma chérie,
> Mon trésor…Mon amour!
> Mon coeur ne vous quitta jamais une seconde,
> Et je suis et serai jusque dans l'autre monde
> Celui qui vous aima sans mesure, celui…

A Few Cyranotes on Casting

There are a number of casting combinations that can be devised for *Cyrano*. Here is a scheme based on The Shakespeare Theatre production. A minimum of 21 actors is required, but the cast can readily be enlarged.

Actor 1 (m): Cyrano de Bergerac

Actor 2 (f): Roxane

Actor 3 (m): Christian de Neuvillette

Actor 4 (m): Ragueneau

Actor 5 (m): Comte de Guiche

Actor 6 (m): Le Bret

Actor 7 (m): Bellerose/Apprentice 3/Capuchin Monk/Spaniard

Actor 8 (m): Montfleury/Voice of Jodelet/Apprentice 2/Spaniard

Actor 9 (f): Duenna/Mother Marguerite

Actor 10 (m): Vicomte de Valvert/Man of Letters/Spaniard

Actor 11 (m): Cut-Purse/Apprentice 1/Sentry

Actor 12 (m): Musketeer 1/Spaniard

Actor 13 (m): Musketeer 2/Cadet 7

Actor 14 (f): Orange Girl/Sister Marthe

Actor 15 (f): Lisa/Sister Claire

Actor 16 (f): Musician 1/Page 1/Cadet 5/Sister 1
with Musical Instrument

Actor 17 (m): Musician 2/Page 2/Cadet 6/Sister 2
with Musical Instrument

Actor 18 (m): Cadet 1

Actor 19 (m): Cadet 2

Actor 20 (m): Cadet 3

Actor 21 (m): Cadet 4

Because the world depicted on stage in *Cyrano* is not intended to be a fully realistic one, the play allows some flexibility in casting regarding the gender of the actors. There are roles that can be played by either sex without altering a word of text. Examples include the Musicians of Scene 1, the Apprentices in Scene 2, and the Pages from Scene 3. Any or all of the Nuns in the final scene can be played in drag, and directors may choose to have female actors portray some of the Cadets of Gascony. Such changes may help to better balance the company by gender if so desired, and still permit the doubling of roles, thereby not enlarging cast size.

Pronunciation Guide

Below is a guide to the pronunciation of some of the French names of people, places, titles and phrases used in this adaptation. (The list is not inclusive.) For the most part, French names have been Anglicized. The only exceptions are for those names that are too familiar to American ears in their original language (such as the "Porte Saint Denis"—"*Den-ee*"—which is a Paris landmark, and "Corneille"—"*Corn-nay*," the landmark author) and those that would just sound too "gauche" if Anglicized (for example: "Jodelet" which should be pronounced "*Jo-duh-lay*," not "jo-duh-LET"). The following are listed in alphabetical order.

Bellerose = *Bell-uh-rose*
Bourgogne = *Bor-gog-nya*
Ca peu = *sah pyu*
Comte de Guiche = *Comt duh Geesh*
Corneille = *Corn-nay*
Denis = *Den-ee*
de trop = *duh tro*
épée = *eh-pay*
Gascon = *Gaz-cone*
Gascony = *Gas-cone-ee*
Jodelet = *Jo-duh-lay*
Le Bret = *Luh Bret*
Lise = *Lees*
Madeleine = *Mad-ah-lane*
mal de mer = *mowl-duh-mare*
Montfleury = *Mont-flur-ee*
Neuvillette = *Nu-vuh-LET or Nu-vuh-YET*
                        (Company's choice)
Ragueneau = *Rag-guh-no*
sous = *soo*
Vicomte de Valvert = *Vee-comt duh Val-ver(t)*

DIRECTOR'S NOTES

DIRECTOR'S NOTES